M
IS
THE ANSWER
FOR
EVERYTHING

By Joseph Willis
Sydneyicc.org

This labor of love is dedicated to God's glory, my adorable wife Kerry, my precious children Ally and Luke, and to my beloved and generous Sydney International Christian Church Family.

Acknowledgements

Every man starts as a blank canvas and is molded by those around him. When it comes to my views on wealth, the most profound by far has been my father with his never-ending generosity and hospitality. Thank you, Dad.

Of course, thanks be to God, who called me at the age of 23 to follow Him and has never stopped fine-tuning that foundation for His purposes. I had the joy of falling in love with Him in 1990 and the adventure has never stopped. I pray He is proud of me.

Those I believe deserve the most acknowledgement are they who have had to live with me constantly practicing this book's content on their lives. Namely my amazing wife Kerry and our incredible kids, Luke and Ally. The decisions I have made for God and His Kingdom have often forced sacrifices on them that they would never have otherwise made. It has meant them going without on numerous occasions, having to leave schools, friends, even countries… all in the name of God and His Kingdom. Yet God has rewarded them every single time.

A huge thank you to everyone in the Sydney International Christian Church, who have been my ultimate "guinea pigs", as I have preached the Scriptures and convictions laid out in this book to them. We wrestled with God together on numerous occasions striving to apply practicals to these Biblical principles. I believe that you have become the most generous group that God has given me the privilege to lead.

Last but by no means least, thank you to Kip McKean. You not only helped me to meticulously edit this book over the weekend that the Spirit launched the Hong Kong International Christian

Church. I want to also thank you for your courage to call yourself and everyone you know to emphatically follow God's Word. Thank you for your friendship, mentoring, vision, patience and discipling. It is an honor beyond words to be led by a man of vision, in a world where so few have it.

To all my other friends who have made me the man I am today and the countless SoldOut Movement Disciples whose financial sacrifices have not only birthed the Sydney Church but all the other congregations in our family of churches, my deepest gratitude. **"We are family… to the end!"**

Joe Willis
September 3, 2017

Introduction

When God through King Solomon wrote that *"money is the answer for everything"* (Ecclesiastes 10:19), he was not saying that money saves you or makes you happy, as these are gifts from God. However, as a man who had much wealth, he understood what could be achieved with money. He undertook many building projects where he must have encountered a variety of problems, but he understood that financial resources can compensate for lack of skill or time.

What is one of the biggest challenges in the church today? It is the same as in Jesus's day and the days of the early church:

> *[Jesus] told them, "The harvest is plentiful, but the workers are few. Ask the Lord of the harvest, therefore, to send out workers into His harvest field."* (Luke 10:2)

There are many people that God has prepared for salvation but few workers who are out there doing the work. While it is every Christian's purpose to seek and save the lost, there is a direct correlation between the growth of a church and the number of competent full-time ministry staff. Men and women need to be freed up to be trained in how to do the ministry, to learn on the job how to build churches, and to shepherd souls. Consequently, men and women need the funds to lead groups and churches, as well as to be missionaries establishing new churches.

Jesus knew that He needed to be free of work as did the men He trained, so that He could totally focus on training His disciples before He died. To do that, they were supported by other disciples including several women. (Luke 8:2-3) Today we need many men and women dedicated full-time to forcefully advance God's Kingdom. Regarding building His Kingdom and the full-time workers supported, this book addresses the issue of convincing every reader that we should not simply give financially to feel good about ourselves or to tithe to feel like our duty is done. Instead as Jesus taught, we need to give up everything for the sake of saving the world; this includes living a life where our wealth is used purposefully to fuel the advancement of God's Kingdom not our own desires and comfort, which only leads to a lack of saved souls. (Luke 14:33; Mark 4:18-19)

This leads me to the focus of the first nine chapters of this book and the heart of the matter. For every person that gives money to God and His cause there are different struggles. For some, they must deal with a lack of faith or with greed in their hearts and life. While others, they must abandon wrong teachings or limiting doctrines that they picked up over their years. The reason for writing this book is to help you to evaluate some of these issues and see if there is a need to change your heart when it comes to your views and beliefs about money and God.

The second section of the book focusses more on practicals regarding money. These have been written in answer to the many questions asked over the years about a myriad of issues, such as how to teach others clearly about money, also what to do with money and when.

I have had the privilege of supporting those in the ministry half of my Christian life. Twice, I have had the opportunity to finance myself in the full-time ministry, and on three occasions I have been supported by others. This has allowed me to see and struggle with the issues of giving and being given to by people.

Three primary things have helped me surrender my wealth to God. First, I was brought up in a generous family with a father who typified generosity to others, even when he could not really afford it. Second, for many years, I have been part of a church that unashamedly called everyone to give up everything to save the world in our generation. Third, God has put me in tight financial situations again and again, so that I have had to learn to trust Him, only to see God lavish His support on me and those that I have led. This in turn has enabled me, as well as my ministries, to give generously to others.

The first nine chapters of this book are purposefully written in a style so that they can be used as lessons. The material may be preached or broken down into sections for study in small groups. Chapters 10 to 21 are written in a format of "mini studies" to help to answer commonly asked questions and to solve frequent issues in Christians lives today.

Table Of Contents

Acknowledgements

Introduction

Section IV: Mini Studies

Chapter 10 Dealing With Money And Contribution At Conversion

Chapter 11 Fulfilling Your Contribution Pledge To God

Chapter 12 Increasing Your Giving

Chapter 13 Our Responsibility To The Poor

Chapter 14 Budgeting And Managing Your Money

Chapter 15 Providing For Your Family

Chapter 16 Buying A House And Inheriting Houses

Chapter 17 What Career Should I Choose?

Chapter 18 How To Make Money

Chapter 19 Savings, Retirement And Leaving An Inheritance

Chapter 20 Lending, Borrowing Money, And Dealing With Debts

Chapter 21 Should I Pay Taxes To An Unjust Government?

Conclusion

SECTION ONE
THE HEART OF THE MATTER

Chapter 1
It Is All About The Heart

Introduction

Teacher, which is the greatest commandment in the Law? Jesus replied: "Love the Lord your God with all your heart and with all your soul and with all your mind." This is the first and greatest commandment. And the second is like it: "Love your neighbor as yourself." All the Law and the Prophets hang on these two commandments. (Matthew 22:36-40)

When it comes to giving our money to God and His Kingdom, it's all about the heart. Ideally, our hearts should be set on loving God and other people, either God's children or the lost. When we forget that and look at money from a selfish perspective, it will lead us to ungodliness.

Being asked to give money or possessions is not what makes us struggle; it simply exposes where we are struggling. This is seen throughout the individual accounts in the Bible such as the Rich Ruler (Luke 18:18-30), Judas - one of the Twelve Apostles (John 12:4-6), and Ananias and Sapphira. (Acts 5:1-11)

Does God really need our money? In one sense no. If you are not willing to give, God can secure it from someone else or somewhere else. God's Kingdom does not rely upon us as an individual; it is we who desperately need His Kingdom for love, support and encouragement. Think about how much wealth is at God's disposal. He could guide the outcome of a national lottery to be given to someone who could then donate it all to His Kingdom. Yet would that "really" help our hearts? (It would help mine to some degree you might cry!)

As a parent, one of the most treasured gifts given to my wife Kerry was a Yugio trading card from my son when he was eight years old. He loved the game and the TV series, we played the card game often. When Kerry's birthday came up, my son chose his favorite and most valuable card, and proudly presented it to my wife for her birthday. Did my wife play or understand the game? No! Did my son even buy the card in the first place? No! I bought it for him in one of our times together. What was the monetary value of the card? Hardly anything. Yet what moved my wife's heart and my heart was that our son had given the possession of greatest value to him as a willing gesture of the love he had for his mum.

That is all God wants, our hearts. When we understand that and act like that, we will not only move God's heart, but we will also never struggle in giving up any amount of money or any possession to Him, our Father.

Point I: The History Of Contribution To God Before The Law

A. Abel Versus Cain – The Best Versus Some

> *In the course of time, Cain brought some of the fruits of the soil as an offering to the Lord. But Abel brought fat portions from some of the firstborn of his flock. The Lord looked with favor on Abel and his offering, but on Cain and his offering He did not look with favor. So Cain was very angry, and his face was downcast.* (Genesis 4:3-5)

The very first occasion that men made an offering to God, two very different hearts were revealed. Abel brought the most valued part of his prized possessions, the fat of his firstborn, and Cain just brought *"some"* of what he had. In these two men, we see reflected the hearts of all men and women who come to God with offerings. Those like Abel think about what they are doing when they bring their offering and to whom they are bringing it. They consider how much God means to them, how much God has given to them, and how much He deserves thanks and gratitude. Those like Cain just give some. They give because they know it is the right thing to do, yet their lack of gratitude and understanding of how God provides for them, inevitably will lead them to offer only some. How did God view Cain's offering of giving just some? He viewed it as evil!

> *Do not be like Cain, who belonged to the evil one and murdered his brother. And why did he murder him? Because his own actions were evil and his brother's were righteous.* (1 John 3:12)

To treat God – the Author of our life and our ultimate Father – with contempt is evil. God is very clear throughout the Bible that we are to give our fathers honor, respect and deep love, and all the more so our Father God.

B. Noah – Is Your First Thought To Give Back To God?

Noah, with his family, survived the great flood that killed so many. He is one of the few saved and when he comes out of the ark with his family, what do you think he does? Throw a party? Set about organizing everything? No, his first thought is to give back to God.

> *Then Noah built an altar to the Lord and, taking some of all the clean animals and clean birds, he sacrificed burnt offerings on it. The Lord smelled the pleasing aroma and said in His heart: "Never again will I curse the ground because of man, even though every inclination of his heart is evil from childhood. And never again will I destroy all living creatures, as I have done."* (Genesis 8:20-21)

What is amazing about Noah's deed is how it moved God's heart to make an eternal promise of grace. In Noah, God saw a heart that He valued. Even if billions of people in the future would not make God feel loved, He was willing to bear with that fact in the hope of the few like Noah.

We must check our hearts when we are blessed with possessions, money, gifts, wage, increases, etc. Our first thought should be to give back to God before we go about the distractions of our daily lives.

C. Abraham – Initiating Giving Back To God Through God's Representative

After a great victory against the odds while rescuing his nephew Lot, Abraham is approached by a priest of God proclaiming that his success was from God and not from his own strength or intellect. What was his reaction?

> *Then Melchizedek king of Salem brought out bread and wine. He was priest of God Most High, and he blessed Abram, saying, "Blessed be Abram by God Most High, Creator of Heaven and earth. And blessed be God Most High, who delivered your enemies into your hand." Then Abram gave him a tenth of everything.* (Genesis 14:18-20)

Abraham had the heart to initiate giving a financial sacrifice to God's representative without any suggestion or prompting. He saw it as giving to God himself. He gave him a "one-off payment" of a tenth of all his plunder. Thank God for the example of spiritual men and women like Abraham in our lives, who remind us where our wealth comes from, so we can make sure we deal with our wealth in a godly manner.

D. Jacob – Appreciative Of God's Protection

After having an encounter with God in a dream, God told Jacob that He would care for him and that He would use Jacob powerfully, what was Jacob's reaction? He was suddenly hit by the reality that God was watching him and that made him a little afraid.

> *Then Jacob made a vow, saying, "If God will be with me and will watch over me on this journey I am taking and will give me food to eat and clothes to wear so that I return safely to my father's house, then the Lord will be my God and this stone that I have set up as a pillar will be God's house, and of all that you give me I will give you a tenth.*
> (Genesis 28:20-22)

Jacob made a vow of his own free will that would help remind him that he should always be aware of God in his life and have a holy fear of God. What better way than giving a portion of every piece of wealth he received? Not just a portion of a wage, but a percentage of everything every day, every week, every year to focus him on God whenever any and every blessing came his way.

You can surmise that the Law given to the nation of Israel was based upon the great hearts of these men before the Law: Abel, Noah, Abraham and Jacob.

> *Set apart for the Lord your God every firstborn male of your herds and flocks. Do not put the firstborn of your oxen to work, and do not shear the firstborn of your sheep.*
> (Deuteronomy 15:19; Deuteronomy 18:1-5)

> *Honor the Lord with your wealth, with the firstfruits of all your crops; then your barns will be filled to overflowing, and*

your vats will brim over with new wine. (Proverbs 3:9-10)

I give to the Levites all the tithes in Israel as their inheritance in return for the work they do while serving at the Tent of Meeting. (Numbers 18:21)

Be sure to set aside a tenth of all that your fields produce each year. Eat the tithe of your grain, new wine and oil, and the firstborn of your herds and flocks in the presence of the Lord your God at the place He will choose as a dwelling for His Name, so that you may learn to revere the Lord your God always. (Deuteronomy 14:22-23)

The spirit of the Law was before the Law, and the spirit of the Law is what should be our focus today, not the Law itself. The Law has been abolished by Christ (Colossians 2:14), because it was and always will be about heart.

Point II: God Wants Your Heart Not Your Money

A. God Builds His Dwelling Place With Only Willing People

A prime example of this is seen in the making of God's Tabernacle:

The Lord said to Moses, "Tell the Israelites to bring me an offering. You are to receive the offering for me from each man whose heart prompts him to give. These are the offerings you are to receive from them: gold, silver and bronze; blue, purple and scarlet yarn and fine linen; goat hair; ram skins dyed red and hides of sea cows; acacia wood; olive oil for the light; spices for the anointing oil and for the fragrant incense; and onyx stones and other gems to be mounted on the ephod and breastpiece. Then have them make a sanctuary for me, and I will dwell among them. Make this Tabernacle and all its furnishings exactly like the pattern I will show you." (Exodus 25:1-9)

The Tabernacle was the portable dwelling place for God among His people during the time of Israel's journey through the desert and into the Promised Land. In building this sacred dwelling, God only desired gifts that were given willingly. This was also the case for all the objects inside the Tabernacle. God told Moses they were only to be made from contributions willingly given. (Exodus 35:4-5) Moses sent out the command and only those who had willing hearts and whose hearts were moved came with their wealth.

> *Then the whole Israelite community withdrew from Moses' presence, and everyone who was willing and whose heart moved him came and brought an offering to the Lord for the work on the Tent of Meeting, for all its service, and for the sacred garments.* (Exodus 35:20-21)

This same quality of being "willing" was applied to all those who were to help build the Sanctuary for God.

> *So Bezalel, Oholiab and every skilled person to whom the Lord has given skill and ability to know how to carry out all the work of constructing the Sanctuary are to do the work just as the Lord has commanded. Then Moses summoned Bezalel and Oholiab and every skilled person to whom the Lord had given ability and who was willing to come and do the work. They received from Moses all the offerings the Israelites had brought to carry out the work of constructing the Sanctuary. And the people continued to bring freewill offerings morning after morning. So all the skilled craftsmen who were doing all the work on the Sanctuary left their work and said to Moses, "The people are bringing more than*

enough for doing the work the Lord commanded to be done." Then Moses gave an order and they sent this word throughout the camp: "No man or woman is to make anything else as an offering for the Sanctuary." And so the people were restrained from bringing more, because what they already had was more than enough to do all the work.
(Exodus 36:1-7)

B. God Only Wants The Willing In His Church

The equivalent of the Tabernacle today, the place where God lives on earth, is His church - the Kingdom of God. He works through men and women to build His church with their wealth and their efforts. God only wants to work through those who are "willing" to give their finances, their possessions, their time, their efforts and ultimately their hearts. Today the sacrifice and love of Jesus is our motivation to give above and beyond what may seem normal and right, like when the Israelites gave their sacrifices to build the Tabernacle.

For Christ's love compels us, because we are convinced that one died for all, and therefore all died. And He died for all, that those who live should no longer live for themselves but for Him who died for them and was raised again.
(2 Corinthians 5:14-15)

In Heaven, God only wants to be surrounded by those who want to be there and spend eternity worshipping Him willingly. How horrible it would be in Heaven if some did not want to be there or were half-hearted. It is the same in His Kingdom on earth, His church.

Each man should give what he has decided in his heart to

give, not reluctantly or under compulsion, for God loves a cheerful giver. (2 Corinthians 9:7)

God loves a willing heart, not a reluctant heart. So, if you do not have a willing heart, you must sort this out as a matter of urgency, because where your heart is will determine if your gift is acceptable to God.

C. Only Give Acceptably

For if the willingness is there, the gift is acceptable according to what one has, not according to what he does not have. (2 Corinthians 8:12)

To give without being wholehearted is not just a little issue, it is detestable to God. This is seen when the people of Israel gave animal sacrifices that possibly from the outside looked all right, but on closer inspection had defects or flaws.

Do not sacrifice to the Lord your God an ox or a sheep that has any defect or flaw in it, for that would be detestable to Him. (Deuteronomy 17:1)

The issue when your heart is not willing to give is not to refrain from giving, but to sort your heart out quickly and then give. You cannot use your sin as an excuse to not be godly. An unwilling heart in one area will either lead to unwillingness in other areas or is a symptom of you not doing well in other spiritual areas of your life. As with Cain when his heart was not fully committed to giving God his best, God challenged him to master his sin. (Genesis 4:7)

Point III: The Real Reasons Why We Struggle To Give

There have been times in my life when I struggled to give my weekly contribution, even one-off contributions, special contributions, raising money for missions and even for the poor. It is the same question I am always asked, either by my conscience or by another disciple, "Are you happy to give, or is there a reluctance, reservation or even a bitterness to give?"

Here are some of the thought patterns that either I or my dear brothers and sisters have shared when we were not doing well spiritually to try and justify why we should not give. There are also some Scriptures that address how to overcome our wrong thinking.

A. People

1. I feel hurt by someone (or just do not like someone): another disciple, a leader, my mentor or discipling partner, and until they resolve this with me, I am not giving. That way I will get the attention I desire. (Matthew 5:21-25)

2. I feel like it is the church not God asking for this. Is God really behind this? (Leviticus 7:11-14)

3. I do not feel like I was listened to or consulted on the amount needed or being given, so until I do I will withhold my money. (1 Peter 2:23; Hebrews 13:17)

4. I do not trust people, especially a few of the leaders in my local congregation and sometimes those overseeing my church, so I will not give or give all I should. (Acts 4:34-35; 1 Corinthians 13:6-7)

5. I will give a good amount, so no one challenges me, but not what I know I should. (Acts 5:1-11)

B. Circumstance

1. I cannot afford to give. If I give, I am not sure that I will have enough money to pay my bills, rent, debts, etc. (Philippians 4:19)

2. My non-Christian family needs the money more than God's church. (Matthew 12:48-50)

3. I am thinking about leaving the church, so I am not going to give.
(2 Chronicles 16:9)
4. I have overspent this week, so I cannot give. (Deuteronomy 23:23)
5. I think I am losing my job, so I need the money and cannot give.
(Proverbs 3:5-6)

C. Doctrine

1. I prefer to give to the poor. The church will do fine without the money, and I like giving to the poor more. (Matthew 6:33)
2. I already give a tithe and that is enough. (Luke 14:33)
3. God does not care if I withhold my money and it will not affect me.
(Ecclesiastes 5:4-6; Proverbs 11:24)
4. I will only give to God if I can afford to after I have paid all my bills.
(Proverbs 3:9-10; Matthew 6:33)
5. I need to see how to work out my finances or I will not give to God what I know I have said I would. (Romans 1:17; Ephesians 3:20)

The problem with all these statements is that they are emotions or reasoning from a human point of view and fail to consider God's perspective on the situation. The real question should be what does God want me to do? Is God testing your faith right now? Is your love for Him being questioned or attacked by Satan just like in the Book of Job? Is Satan trying to put doubts in your mind like, "Does God truly love me?" That is exactly how he tempted Eve. Is what I committed to giving yesterday the very best I can give today to the love of my life, God?

God knows your life, your situation, your every intimate detail, and it should be to Him that we go to sort out our heart and ask Him how to respond to any challenges set before us. For example, why has God given these circumstances to us and how does He want us to react to them? We should rely on the love of God (1 John 4:16) to sort out our lives not on our strength or human reasoning. This is done by diligently studying the Scriptures that relate to our situation and heart. Then through extensive prayer, we must resolve the issues with God. Remember prayer is there to get our heart in line with God's heart, not to get God's heart in line with ours. (Mark 14:32-42)

Conclusion

It's all about heart.

1. This is seen in the examples before the Law in Genesis.
2. God is interested in our hearts; He only wants a Kingdom of people with willing hearts.
3. When we really look at the excuses we use to not give our wealth, we see God has given a solution for each problem or issue.

The challenge for us all is to make sure our heart is right before God when it comes to giving our wealth in all its forms.

Chapter 2
Why Do You Want To Be Rich?

Introduction

Why do you want to be rich? Jesus did not!

> *For you know the grace of our Lord Jesus Christ, that though He was rich, yet for your sakes He became poor, so that you through His poverty might become rich.* (2 Corinthians 8:9)

The desire for wealth or to be rich was not part of Jesus's character or purpose in life. He gave up incomprehensible riches in Heaven to come to Earth and live a life of poverty. He was born in a stable and lived as a refugee with His parents in Egypt before returning to Israel. Jesus helped His mother provide for His siblings after His father had died and then was supported by women disciples while He wandered the countryside preaching God's Word. He called His disciples to do the same as Peter exclaimed and eventually did.

> *Peter said to Him, "We have left all we had to follow you!"* (Luke 18:28)

> *Then Peter said, "Silver or gold I do not have, but what I have I give you."* (Acts 3:6)

When we look at people with wealth and struggle with envy or jealousy we must ask ourselves why are we feeling that way? To be rich is choosing the hardest path to Heaven. Why would any spiritual person want to do that as being rich is something that Jesus warned against?

> *Jesus looked at him and said, "How hard it is for the rich to enter the Kingdom of God! Indeed, it is easier for a camel to*

go through the eye of a needle than for a rich man to enter the Kingdom of God." (Luke 18:24-25)

But woe to you who are rich, for you have already received your comfort. Woe to you who are well fed now, for you will go hungry. Woe to you who laugh now, for you will mourn and weep. (Luke 6:24-25)

Point I: Blessed Are The Poor

A. Salvation Comes To The Poor

Looking at His disciples, He said: "Blessed are you who are poor, for yours is the Kingdom of God." (Luke 6:20)

The core issue in becoming a Christian is giving up everything for Christ and His Kingdom. What are some of those things? For some their cost is a job; for others giving up their career, moving to a new city, not living in luxury, no longer receiving the praise of men, and the list goes on. All these things cost a lot of money or could potentially lead to gaining a lot of money. The poor have no such hurdles. Those that do are called to live as if they do not, to become poor by giving up everything. And when Jesus says everything, He means everything!

In the same way, those of you who do not give up everything you have cannot be my disciples. (Luke 14:33)

The blessings for the poor, and especially those who choose poverty over wealth like Moses, is that they will see the Kingdom flourish in their generation and will be with Moses in Heaven.

[Moses] chose to be mistreated along with the people of God rather than to enjoy the pleasures of sin for a short

time. He regarded disgrace for the sake of Christ as of greater value than the treasures of Egypt, because he was looking ahead to his reward. (Hebrews 11:25-26)

Also, study out the story of Lazarus in Luke 16:19-31.

B. Rich In Faith

Listen, my dear brothers: Has not God chosen those who are poor in the eyes of the world to be rich in faith and to inherit the Kingdom He promised those who love Him? (James 2:5)

I know your afflictions and your poverty, yet you are rich! (Revelation 2:9a)

Most Christians want to be men and women of great faith, yet for that to occur you need to be in position where great faith is needed. For example, like Daniel trusting in God in the lion's den (Daniel 6) or his friends Shadrach, Meshach and Abednego standing up to their king in the name of God. (Daniel 3) All these men needed to rely completely on the love and power of God to rescue them, and when He did, their faith and the faith of those around them soared.

So it is with the poor. Being poor by nature means that you must rely on God to help you. You often cannot see the solution to how you will provide for yourself or your family, your friends or your church. When God provides again and again, your faith is built not only in this area of your life, but in all areas of your life. The rich do not have this "privilege" of growing in their faith because they do not need to be rescued financially as they are their own rescuers. Two poor widows come to mind: The widow giving her last two coins she had to live on, to God at the Temple, trusting He would provide for her (Luke 21:1-4); and the prophet's widow, who was left in such debt by her husband that she was facing the possibility of selling her sons.

(2 Kings 4:1-7) These women had to first be in desperate need for them to see their need for God. In turn, God took care of them.

I have had the privilege of seeing God work powerfully in the SoldOut Movement Church Family. Remarkably so in the last 11 years, as 91 churches have been planted in 36 nations all being financially fueled by Christians who were willing to become poor in this world! Of these, many have given upward of 20% of their yearly income, several 30%, and even some above this to see the world won for Christ. A number sold property and businesses to give money for mission teams that would otherwise have been delayed. Yes, this has made them poor, stressed and stretched many times, but through it all they have become rich in faith. Ask them if it was money well sacrificed as they have seen their friends, family, work colleagues and complete strangers have their lives changed by God's Word and you will hear a loud YES!

Poverty with God is not something to be feared. In fact, it is something we should embrace as any other challenge. We must see it as an opportunity for God to display His love and power in our lives.

Consider it pure joy, my brothers and sisters, whenever you face trials of many kinds, because you know that the testing of your faith produces perseverance. Let perseverance finish its work so that you may be mature and complete, not lacking anything. If any of you lacks wisdom, you should ask God, who gives generously to all without finding fault, and it will be given to you. But when you ask, you must believe and not doubt, because the one who doubts is like a wave of the sea, blown and tossed by the wind. That person should not expect to receive anything from the Lord. Such a person is double-minded and unstable in all they do.

Believers in humble circumstances ought to take pride in their high position. But the rich should take pride in their humiliation since they will pass away like a wild flower. (James 1:2-10)

C. The Freedom Of Poverty

A man's riches may ransom his life, but a poor man hears no threat. (Proverbs 13:8)

During my late 30's and early 40's, I bought into the worldly dream of a big house, a financially rewarding career, and saving for retirement. I purchased for myself a good car and one for my wife, as well as gadgets for the kids. Then we experienced two things that made me see just how financially unstable I was. First a cyclone that was later declared a national disaster, hit our neighborhood ripping up houses and blew out our windows. My family and I were in the house and caught in the actual eye of the storm and there was nothing we could do. Here we had been spending time building our house and our garden, yet in a moment – 20 minutes – our garden was ripped apart and the house was badly damaged.

Secondly was being in the middle of a financial recession where my peers lost their jobs. As a senior manager in a company, I had to make people redundant and I did not know if I was going to be able to pay my mortgage the next month. One year later, we had sold our house to finance ourselves to move from Australia to America to train for the ministry. We now live in rented houses, with the remainder of the goods we originally had, plus goods gathered from the side of the street. We feel no threat of losing our house because we do not have one. We feel no threat of not being able to pay our bills as they are temporary bills, and if hard times hit, we could always move in with generous disciples. Now we are in a sold-out church with Biblical convictions that are being lived out daily. We do not talk about housing interest rates going up or down. We are living day to day trusting God with our future and free of worry about future circumstances.

Point II: Dangers Of Wealth

A. Wealth Is Deceitful

> *Do not wear yourself out to get rich; have the wisdom to show restraint. Cast but a glance at riches, and they are gone, for they will surely sprout wings and fly off to the sky like an eagle.* (Proverbs 23:4-5)

Money is an unreliable friend. I have seen my own father save for retirement diligently as he was taught by his peers, the financial advisors of his day, and countless television adverts only to see it all nearly lost in a stock market crash. Sadly, he still must work in his 80's. (Also, see Proverbs 18:11; Proverbs 27:23-24; Ecclesiastes 5:13-14; 1 Timothy 6:17; and Proverbs 11:28.)

Money cannot buy you spirituality. Consider the case of Simon the Sorcerer:

> *When Simon saw that the Spirit was given at the laying on of the Apostles' hands, he offered them money and said, "give me also this ability so that everyone on whom I lay my hands may receive the Holy Spirit." Peter answered: "May your money perish with you, because you thought you could buy the gift of God with money!"* (Acts 8:18-20)

Money can also lead you to thinking that you are spiritual when you are not, as in the case of Ephraim.

Ephraim boasts, "I am very rich; I have become wealthy. With all my wealth they will not find in me any iniquity or sin." (Hosea 12:8)

Yet in Hosea 12:1, God says about Ephraim that they are full of lies and violence. It is taught by some that personal financial blessing for your own desires shows proof that you are righteous, which doctrinally goes totally against Jesus's teaching in the Parable of the Rich Man and Lazarus (Luke 16:22-23), as well as many other Scriptures.

B. Money Does Not Make You Happy

The sleep of a laborer is sweet, whether he eats little or much, but the abundance of a rich man permits him no sleep. (Ecclesiastes 5:12)

Solomon amassed silver and gold yet found it meaningless. (Ecclesiastes 2) Wealth is empty without God, without His purposes. Many rich people are unhappy even to the point of suicide, as seen in the case of Judas. Judas knew Jesus, God in the flesh personally. Judas saw amazing miracles, people healed before his very eyes and witnessed lives changed. He heard new teachings that stirred souls and brought comfort, yet all this was not enough. You must ask yourselves why? He loved money and deep-down thought it was the solution that would bring him and others happiness. If money was not his motive, he would simply have betrayed Jesus with no financial gain. That is why he was a thief. For him, God was not enough. He had the appearance of spirituality, an Apostle no less, yet that was not enough.

But one of His disciples, Judas Iscariot, who was later to betray Him, objected, "Why wasn't this perfume sold and the money given to the poor? It was worth a year's wages."' He did not say this because he cared about the poor but because he was a thief; as keeper of the money bag, he used to help himself to what was put into it. (John 12:4-6)

It was after Judas saw Mary of Bethany, in his view, waste money on an unworthy cause that he then betrayed Jesus to the chief priests. (Matthew 26:6-16) Again, Judas' heart was revealed as he did not simply want to betray Jesus, so he asked the Jewish leaders, "What's in it for me?"

Judas asked, "What are you willing to give me if I hand him over to you?" So they counted out for him thirty silver coins. (Matthew 26:15)

Did the money bring him happiness? NO! Later, Judas was full of remorse for what he had done and even tried to give the money back (Matthew 27:3-5), but ultimately his love of money led not only to his spiritual death, but also to him hanging himself. As Solomon said:

Whoever loves money never has enough; whoever loves wealth is never satisfied with their income. This too is meaningless. (Ecclesiastes 5:10)

The scariest thing for me about the case of Judas is that Jesus knew he loved money more than Him. Jesus knew he was a thief, yet as far as we know He did not challenge him on it. Instead, Jesus expected Judas to reveal his heart in confession and deal with it himself, just like we are to do today.

C. Wealth Can Lead You Away From God And His Mission

But godliness with contentment is great gain. For we brought nothing into the world, and we can take nothing out of it. But if we have food and clothing, we will be content with that. People who want to get rich fall into temptation and a trap and into many foolish and harmful desires that plunge men into ruin and destruction. For the love of money is a root of all kinds of evil. Some people, eager for money, have wandered from the faith and pierced themselves with many griefs. (1 Timothy 6:6-10)

One of the worst things that can happen to us is to chase money and get it, becoming rich. The more money that we have, the more things we buy; subsequently, the more time we spend playing with or maintaining these new possessions. This eats into the time we could be spending with God and focused on being fruitful.

Getting rich, being rich, and staying rich consumes our time, choking our ability to save the world. (Mark 4:18-19; Luke 8:14) Success can also make you think more highly of yourself than you should, and wealth can often lead to becoming proud (Ezekiel 28:5), which in turn can lead us to forget God altogether.

But I am the Lord your God, who brought you out of Egypt. You shall acknowledge no God but me, no Savior except me. I cared for you in the desert, in the land of burning heat. When I fed them, they were satisfied; when they were satisfied, they became proud; then they forgot me. (Hosea 13:4-6)

I am in my early 50's now and have been a Christian over 28 years. Sadly, nearly all my friends who were at one-time Christians have stopped being Christians. There were a few who left God in the first couple of years of me becoming a disciple through persecution or other issues, but for the most part, most of them were seduced by success in the world. They were married, bought houses, attained good jobs, and then they drifted into fruitlessness. The mission of saving the world became less and less important to them until they minimized it to a good idea that they rarely practiced. They gave it up as their true focus in life once they had become comfortable. They were having their emotional needs met by their spouse, children, careers and were no longer looking to God for love and comfort to their later demise. (Hosea 10:1-2) It is my heartfelt prayer that they return to the riches of God and His Kingdom and once again embrace Jesus's mission. (Luke 19:10)

Point III: Jesus Teaching On Money And Wealth

Jesus taught so much about money, wealth and riches. Here are just some of His teachings.

A. Love God And Hate Money

> *No servant can serve two masters. Either he will hate the one and love the other, or he will be devoted to the one and despise the other. You cannot serve both God and Money. The Pharisees, who loved money, heard all this and were sneering at Jesus. He said to them, "You are the ones who justify yourselves in the eyes of men, but God knows your hearts. What is highly valued among men is detestable in God's sight."* (Matthew 6:24-25)

B. Do Not Store Up Your Wealth

> *Do not store up for yourselves treasures on earth, where moth and rust destroy, and where thieves break in and steal. But store up for yourselves treasures in Heaven, where moth and rust do not destroy, and where thieves do not break in and steal. For where your treasure is, there your heart will be also.* (Matthew 6:19-21)

Sell your possessions and give to the poor. Provide purses for yourselves that will not wear out, a treasure in Heaven that will not be exhausted, where no thief comes near and no moth destroys. (Luke 12:33)

Then [Jesus] said to them, "Watch out! Be on your guard against all kinds of greed; a man's life does not consist in the abundance of his possessions."
And He told them this parable: "The ground of a certain rich man produced a good crop. He thought to himself, 'What shall I do? I have no place to store my crops.'
"Then he said, 'This is what I'll do. I will tear down my barns and build bigger ones, and there I will store all my grain and my goods. And I'll say to myself, "You have plenty of good things laid up for many years. Take life easy; eat, drink and be merry."
"But God said to him, 'You fool! This very night your life will be demanded from you. Then who will get what you have prepared for yourself?'
"This is how it will be with anyone who stores up things for himself but is not rich toward God." (Luke 12:15-21)

C. Do Not Worry About Having Your Needs Met

Then Jesus said to His disciples: "Therefore I tell you, do not worry about your life, what you will eat; or about your body, what you will wear. Life is more than food, and the body more than clothes. Consider the ravens: They do not sow or reap, they have no storeroom or barn; yet God feeds them. And how much more valuable you are than birds! Who of you by worrying can add a single hour to his life? Since you cannot do this very little thing, why do you worry about the rest? Consider how the lilies grow. They do not labor or spin. Yet I tell you, not even Solomon in all his splendor was dressed like one of these. If that is how God clothes the grass of the field, which is here today, and tomorrow is thrown into the fire, how much more will he clothe you, O you of little faith! And do not set your heart on what you will eat or drink; do not worry about it. For the pagan world runs after all such things, and your Father knows that you need them. But seek His Kingdom, and these things will be given to you as well." (Luke 12:22-31)

D. Give

Jesus expects us to give to the needy. It is not an option, that is why He says, *"When you give to the needy."* So, it is not "if" you give to the needy, but "when" you give to those less fortunate.

Be careful not to do your "acts of righteousness" before men, to be seen by them. If you do, you will have no reward from your Father in Heaven.

So when you give to the needy, do not announce it with trumpets, as the hypocrites do in the synagogues and on the streets, to be honored by men. I tell you the truth, they have received their reward in full. But WHEN you give to the needy, do not let your left hand know what your right hand is doing, so that your giving may be in secret. Then your Father, who sees what is done in secret, will reward you. (Matthew 6:1-4)

I tell you, use worldly wealth to gain friends for yourselves, so that when it is gone, you will be welcomed into eternal dwellings. (Luke 16:9)

E. Learn To Handle Worldly Wealth Well

Whoever can be trusted with very little can also be trusted with much, and whoever is dishonest with very little will also be dishonest with much. So if you have not been trustworthy in handling worldly wealth, who will trust you with true riches? And if you have not been trustworthy with someone else's property, who will give you property of your own? (Luke 16:10-15)

F. Give Up Everything

In the same way, any of you who does not give up everything he has cannot be my disciple. (Luke 14:33)

When Jesus said, *"give up everything,"* He really meant everything!

Conclusion

So why do you want to be rich when Jesus says...

1. Blessed are the poor not the rich.
2. Money can corrupt the soul and distract you from saving the lost.
3. It simply is not in Jesus's teaching to seek riches.

From the Old to the New Covenant, we are reminded to steer clear of the world's desire to get rich.

A faithful man will be richly blessed, but one eager to get rich will not go unpunished. (Proverbs 28:20)

We must focus on giving up wealth to make others spiritually rich. Does this verse describe you?

Poor, yet making many rich; having nothing, and yet possessing everything. (2 Corinthians 6:10)

Chapter 3
Dealing With Greed: Need Versus Want

Introduction

When I studied the Bible to become a Christian in 1990 and shared the sins that I needed to change, greed was not one that came to mind. I was not overweight. I had few possessions, no home, an income that met my needs and little else. You would not have said I was a greedy person at first glance. But as I look back now, I see my desire for excess possessions was masked by my inability to finically buy them; my desire for new gadgets was masked by my lack of knowledge about how to use them; my desire to earn lots of money was masked by my lack of belief that I could earn a lot; and my high metabolism masked how much I over ate. Over the years, my greed has caught up with me and been exposed as my talents, income and knowledge have increased and my metabolism has decreased. Even in giving financially to God, when I have focused on the Law as opposed to the heart I have seen greed creep into my life just like it did with the Pharisees. They gave a tenth of their wealth yet were full of greed.

> *Jesus said "Woe to you, teachers of the Law and Pharisees, you hypocrites! You give a tenth of your spices – mint, dill and cumin. But you have neglected the more important matters of the Law – justice, mercy and faithfulness. You should have practiced the latter, without neglecting the former. You blind guides! You strain out a gnat but swallow a camel. Woe to you, teachers of the Law and Pharisees, you hypocrites! You clean the outside of the cup and dish, but inside they are full of greed and self-indulgence."*
> (Matthew 23:23-25)

When I first became a Christian, I gave willingly. However, as my salary increased so did my spending. I used the justification that I gave to

God and the church so there was no problem with my over spending and indulgence. As I have come to grips with my sin and God's Word, I now see how deceived I was.

Point I: How Does God View Greed?

A. Not A Hint Of Greed

> *But among you there must not be even a hint of sexual immorality, or of any kind of impurity, or of greed, because these are improper for God's holy people. Nor should there be obscenity, foolish talk or coarse joking, which are out of place, but rather thanksgiving. For of this you can be sure: No immoral, impure or greedy person, such a man is an idolater, has any inheritance in the Kingdom of Christ and of God. Let no one deceive you with empty words, for because of such things God's wrath comes on those who are disobedient.* (Ephesians 5:3-6)

Most Christians today are brought up with a conviction that a hint of sexual immorality is wrong: lusting after the opposite sex, watching movies that have pornographic scenes in them, lewd jokes or dressing provocatively. Yet when it comes to having a conviction on a hint of greed in our lives – the desire to have many clothes, cars, shoes, overeating, desiring to have the latest possessions just because you can – we often find a lack of Biblical conviction among believers. Greed will keep you out of Heaven; it is that serious. Do not be deceived; the world will try and convince you that "greed is good!" Yet greed is a form of worship that TV and magazines constantly promote, suggesting that we should "have more, we deserve more, and we are entitled to a better and easier life." We must always remember that *"friendship with the world is hatred towards God"* (James 4:4).

We must put greed to death because it is idolatry. Let us never forget that idolaltry is something emotionally more important to us than God, His Kingdom and His ways. Do not let others deceive you that it is not that bad. There should not even be a hint!

B. It Angers God

> *I was enraged by his sinful greed; I punished him, and hid my face in anger, yet he kept on in his willful ways.* (Isaiah 57:17)

Greed angers God. Therefore, it should anger us. Most of us are desensitized to greed as it is so widely accepted in the first world. It is commonly used as the prime motivator for gaining most things; better careers, pleasures, possessions and holidays. The world and those in power want you to be greedy; it fuels the economy and is used to get you to work hard at work for the promise of a promotion. Yet, greed pulls people away from relationships, their families, their children, their friends and ultimately God because of all the time spent on the eternally unimportant. When we fail in our jobs and studies, when our employers do not need us any more, or no one wants to employ us, we are thrown out on the rubbish heap of broken dreams. When God looks down on all the earth and sees the destruction greed has had on relationships, the imbalance between the starving millions and the over-fed or unconcerned wealthy, how can He not feel anything but anger at the state of mankind globally? It was the sin for which God destroyed Sodom.

> *Now this was the sin of your sister Sodom: She and her daughters were arrogant, overfed and unconcerned; they did not help the poor and needy. They were haughty and did detestable things before me. Therefore I did away with them as you have seen*. (Ezekiel 16:49-50)

C. He Wants You To Put It To Death

Put to death, therefore, whatever belongs to your earthly nature: sexual immorality, impurity, lust, evil desires and greed, which is idolatry. Because of these, the wrath of God is coming. (Colossians 3:5-6)

Is there any possession, job, house or arranged commitment that you could not give up immediately for the sake of God and His Kingdom? If so, then that thing has become an idol to you. What do you need to do to change that in your life today? Where do you see greed deceiving you in your life?   Food

A good challenge for us all is to sit down with someone who knows us well and does not have a problem speaking the truth to us in love and to ask them where they see greed in our life. We need to open up about our life, our finances and our spending habits, to get some help in putting to death greed – one of the most deceitful of sins. Another good challenge is to imagine at church tomorrow that there was a call to go on a mission team, could you respond to the call? If you were told that you could only take one suitcase with you to that new city and country, and you were being asked to live there for the rest of your life, would it be possible for you to do that? How long would it take to get out of your commitments? Have you borrowed money to buy items such as a car that you could not afford? Did someone deceive you that you needed it? How tied into the world are you? Could you easily pack up your suitcase, and then give the rest of your possessions away and say, *"Here I am Lord, send me?"* (Isaiah 6:8) This challenge is not for the young, but for all Christians of every age. We are to put greed to death in such a way that it never again lives in our lives.

I have always been constantly inspired by those around me who live a life putting to death greed in their lives, whether they are teens, students, singles, marrieds or especially single parents. Among the many is a student in Sydney called James Kwok who is studying to be a doctor. James has top grades and a bright future earning significant money, and yet has made great decisions about how he sees his future, his wealth and his purpose now as a Christian. He is consumed with evangelizing and studying the Bible with people. Although he only has $150 AUS a week to live off, he gives a third of it to advance God's church.

Another inspiring example was a single brother named Paul that I lived with in England some 25 years ago. I was impacted by how he viewed his finances, in fact it was revolutionary to me. Paul simply took his salary, paid his bills, then saw how little he could live on and gave the rest to God. I was amazed as I saw him blessed by God with a wife of a similar heart who had her treasures in spiritual things not worldly things.

Two other such people are my friends Ian and Margot Clague who helped us start the church in Sydney. They were midlife with two daughters in school, while running a business whose clients were in the state of Queensland, Australia. So moving to Sydney would mean losing their clients. They had an affordable home with a very manageable mortgage. Yet God had another plan for their life. This plan did not include building their wealth and comfort, but to sell all, then to move to Sydney a year before the mission team arrived to set up everything so that the team could hit the ground running. In doing so, they lost most of their wealth, their comfort and their security. Ian had to get a new job and new schools were needed for the girls. Despite these challenges, they now look back on seeing so many people having become Christians in Sydney, and see the impact of their decision to constantly live a life to "go anywhere, give up everything, at any time for Christ and His dream." I also have seen God bless that decision with miracles in their lives, such as Ian being approached for a job through Facebook from an old boss from 10 years before, completely out of the blue!

Point II: How Does Greed Damage Us?

A. It Damages Relationships

A greedy man brings trouble to his family, but he who hates bribes will live. (Proverbs 15:27)

It is so easy to find yourself spending too much time at work to earn money to "over provide" for your family or for yourself to purchase possessions that you do not need but simply want. Consequently, you do not spend enough time with your physical or spiritual families. It is so easy to let those around us at work or those we are reaching out to convince us to value possessions, status with the latest gadgets, cars, clothes and a certain lifestyle more than relationships.

A greedy man stirs up dissension, but he who trusts in the Lord will prosper. (Proverbs 28:25)

Dissensions, quarrels, disagreements and discord... It has often been said that the number one thing that people argue over in marriage is money, rooted in the "I want syndrome." (James 4:1-2) We must learn to say no to wants and live within our means. Also, people greedy for position, power and recognition as well as people desiring money and possessions will cause dissensions as they are willing to damage relationships to gain what they so desperately desire. (2 Timothy 4:10)

B. It Makes Us Unfruitful

Still others, like seed sown among thorns, hear the Word; but the worries of this life, the deceitfulness of wealth and the desires for other things come in and choke the Word, making it unfruitful. (Mark 4:18-19)

One way to gauge how much the world has a hold on you is to see how effective you are in bearing fruit. To bear fruit takes focus, emotional commitment, time, desire and hard work. Ask yourself, "Is this time in your life the most effective you have been in bearing fruit? When was the last time you bore fruit?" Time spent chasing career promotions, salary raises, gaining and maintaining possessions can be time taken away from being with God, as well as seeking and saving the lost. Also, greed exposed in being overweight can lose you the respect of non-Christians when you preach the gospel to them.

C. It Kills Us Spiritually

> *Jeshurun [Israel] grew fat and kicked; filled with food, he became heavy and sleek. He abandoned the God who made him and rejected the Rock his Savior.* (Deuteronomy 32:15)

Here it describes how Israel as a nation became fat and over fed. They became accustomed to the "good life" and lost their desire as a nation to have a relationship with God. This is frightening – the desire for comfort on a national scale, especially the desire to get your emotional needs met from food or comfort rather than from God. This will and does lead nations away from God.

Comfort can creep into the heart of anyone. Take the case of Eli. He was the Judge of all Israel, and yet in his comfort as leader, he let sin go unchecked with his sons and himself. In his death, we find that he did not address greed. He not only allowed his sons to take what they wanted when they wanted (1 Samuel 2:12-17), but also had become heavy himself. His being overweight was a sign of unchecked greed.

> *When he mentioned the ark of God, Eli fell backward off his chair by the side of the gate. His neck was broken and he*

died, for he was an old man, and he was heavy. He had led Israel forty years. (1 Samuel 4:18)

Greed damages families. It breeds division in the church and among Christians giving cause to jealousy and envy. If left unchecked, it will take you away from God. Unaddressed, it will lead to a loss of salvation

> *Do you not know that the wicked will not inherit the Kingdom of God? Do not be deceived: Neither the sexually immoral nor idolaters nor adulterers nor male prostitutes nor homosexual offenders nor thieves nor the greedy nor drunkards nor slanderers nor swindlers will inherit the Kingdom of God.* (1 Corinthians 6:9-10)

Point III: What Is Greed?

What is greed and how did we get to the point of so much greed in our society today?

A simple definition for greed is the excessive desire to have, to acquire, to possess or to consume more than one needs or deserves. It is most obviously seen in the outward approach to money, possessions and food or drink. Greed like all sin is deceitful. We live in a society that is permeated by greed and we compare ourselves to the standards of those around us. It is so hard to see greed for what it is. If many around you are overweight due to greed, it is easy to justify in your own mind that your greed is not so bad. If those around you have the latest gadgets, it is tempting to want them yourself, even if you do not need them or cannot afford them. When every one of your friends has a car or two, then it is hard to conceive of how to live like those who do not have one.

> *Then Jesus said to them, "Watch out! Be on your guard*

against all kinds of greed; life does not consist in an abundance of possessions." (Luke 12:15)

There are all kinds of greed. Here are some of the most obvious aspects.

A. Greed In Possessions

So why do we buy over-expensive cars, houses, clothes, top brands, designer labels, etc. as opposed to the basic version that will meet our needs? It is because the world tells us to have more, look better, "you deserve it," "you will be more accepted or liked if you have this or that." It is not God who tells us that. Our economy is built on people consuming more, having more, wanting more. A good question to ask ourselves is, "Are we an advertiser's dream or nightmare?" or "Does the TV or magazines influence our buying?" The media is never going to tell you not to buy, they are simply trying to find a reason to make you believe buying is good. My friend Jeremy Beck homeschools his children and does not have commercial television in his house with adverts. The effect on his children is profound. They do not ask or beg him for the latest toys or gadgets. In fact, when he took them to a toy store to buy them a birthday present, they did not rush to any toys and then beg their father to get them this or that. They went to Jeremy to ask advice on what he thought would be a good toy for them. On his guidance, they chose a toy with an attitude of joy and gratitude for what their father had given them rather than complaining about what they did not have.

I always remember as a young Christian in London going over to one of the more senior Christians in the church for dinner. I was shocked at how sparsely John and his wife Rose lived. Their house was bland and sparse with a distinct lack of possessions. I knew he was not known for his great fashion as he wore the same clothes often. Yet after I visited his house, I understood more of why. It was not because he did not have money or the ability to earn it as he had previously had a successful construction business. He simply chose not to buy into the world's lie that possessions increase the quality of your life.

> *Do not love the world or anything in the world. If anyone loves the world, the love of the Father is not in him. For everything in the world, the cravings of sinful man, the lust of his eyes and the boasting of what he has and does, comes not from the Father but from the world. The world and its desires pass away, but the man who does the will of God lives forever.* (1 John 2:15-17)

While we do not all need to imitate the lifestyle of John the Baptist in camel's hair clothes and eating locusts, we may need to be reminded that there was nothing that made Jesus outwardly attractive to the world (Isaiah 53:2-3), nor did Jesus want there to be. He did not try to impress the world with what He possessed, but rather prayed that all would be attracted to the Word of God and His love for God.

One small practical that has helped me avoid buying more possessions, is by going through all my clothes, shoes, etc. and sorting out any that I have not worn in the past year and giving them away. Then I split my clothes into two piles and put one pile away in a suitcase. When I am feeling like buying new clothes or after six months, I pull out my stored clothes and swap them for the ones I have been wearing. This makes me feel like I have new clothes and helps me not buy new unnecessary things.

Jesus had no problem telling people to sell all their possessions to follow Him and trust that He would provide for them. (Luke 12:33; Luke 18:22) Do not forget that the early disciples sold their possessions to provide for others. (Acts 2:45; Acts 4:32-35)

B. Greed in Money

In the Muppet movie of *A Christmas Carol* by Charles Dickens, there is a line of a song that says, **Oh, Scrooge he loves his money because he thinks it gives him power.**

Wealth is deceitful. (Mark 4:19) People honestly believe it will bring them happiness, security, a better life, more friends and better health. While there is some truth to these thoughts, the actual truth is that money does not bring you spiritual happiness or contentment. Wealth may bring you some security, but it is uncertain (1 Timothy 6:17) and can be lost in a moment through no fault of your own; through war, economic crashes and disasters. Money may provide you better healthcare, but it will not prevent you from dying. It may give you more friends (Proverbs 14:20), but what kind of friends?

> *For the love of money is a root of all kinds of evil. Some people, eager for money, have wandered from the faith and pierced themselves with many griefs.* (I Timothy 6:10)

Loving money for what you think it can do for you is idolatry. (Ephesians 5:5) We are to look to God for Him to meet our needs and learn to be happy with what He has given us.

> *Keep your lives free from the love of money and be content with what you have, because God has said, "Never will I leave you; never will I forsake you." So we say with confidence, "The Lord is my helper; I will not be afraid. What can man do to me?"* (Hebrews 13:5-6)

One of the people that I have seen crucify his greed in the desire for money is my friend Chi Leong. Chi originally comes from China and his parents moved him at ten years old to Chicago to follow the American dream. He was brought up with the belief that life was all about making as much money as you can by trying to make it big in the business world. By the age of 24, he had gained an impressive education, career and had saved $26,000 USD. Yet upon becoming a Christian, Chi surrendered this direction in life and put God first. After a year as a Christian, he gave up his career and used all his savings to move to Sydney and support himself to train as a minister to plant the church in Hong Kong. This sort of change goes against many families' cultural way of thinking. However, the result of Chi's example in Sydney breathed faith into so many Chinese people to help them become Christians. It will also lead to seeing many thousands of people being saved in China and beyond as Chi led the planting of the Hong Kong Church in September 2017.

C. Greed In Food And Pleasure

How much food do we need each day? Prevailing thinking is about 2,000 calories or maybe 2,500 calories. I am no expert and I am sure it is different for everyone, but I would guess it is less than what most of us think. Almost everyone does not think about eating from the stand point of what our need is, but rather what we want. Therein lies the problem: WANT verses NEED. Most of debauchery and greed are rooted in "what do I want now." We get upset or bored and instead of turning to God for comfort and direction through prayer or His Word, we turn to instant gratification through food, television, video games, shopping or just plain sin. We must be proactive in curbing our desires by knowing what our needs are, and then, disciplining ourselves to not fall into greed.

> *...and put a knife to your throat if you are given to gluttony.*
> *Do not crave his delicacies, for that food is deceptive.*
> (Proverbs 23:2-3)

My wife Kerry is a great example of not being greedy with food. She will only eat when she is hungry, and not always eat everything put before her but she often saves it for the next day. If there is not enough food to go around, she will gladly take only a small part or go without. This is so different from the way I was brought up. My sister once said that the people in my family "try and think of things to do between meals," as it was such a focus in our lives. My friend Michael Williamson – who leads the church in London – has great conviction on this type of greed and is also a great example of watching everything he eats. This godly approach shows in his energy levels, his health and in his appearance. Michael knows what to eat to give him energy, eating only "clean," unprocessed food. He chooses carefully where he eats and what he eats. He has conviction from the Scriptures that we would all do well to imitate.

Jesus spoke of His body as *"the Temple"* (John 2:21), and God teaches us that we are to look after our bodies as they are the temple for the Holy Spirit because we were bought at a price. (1 Corinthians 6:19-20) We are to honor God with our bodies by looking after them, so we can use them to further His Kingdom for as long as possible. There are not enough Christians doing God's work as it is, so we cannot afford to have people "bowing out" early due to ill health. Satan would be only too pleased for us to buy into that lie.

Something that helped me understand just how much I ate and spent on food, was by taking a month to only eat freshly made juice that I prepared at home. I also did not buy any drinks while I was out, I simply drank water. These two things highlighted how much unnecessary food I usually ate as I watched those around me buy food when neither they nor I were hungry. It also saved me a lot of money.

D. Greed In Power, Status And Recognition

Most people are insecure in some way. They crave acceptance. They want to be liked, respected, valued and feel like their life has meaning. One of the most difficult things as a Christian is to just be happy in the fact that God loves you and that is enough. Nearly all relationship problems in the church stem from people not being treated the way they want or expect to be treated by others. We recount how hard we have worked or how much we have sacrificed and tell ourselves we should be valued more. But what was the real motive for all the effort? Sure, there is love for God there, but too often it is mixed with impure motives.

> *And I saw that all labor and all achievement spring from man's envy of his neighbor. This too is meaningless, a chasing after the wind.* (Ecclesiastes 4:4)

> *All man's efforts are for his mouth, yet his appetite is never satisfied.* (Ecclesiastes 6:7)

It has been said, "How greedy is the man for whom God is not enough." We can tell if this type of greed is our weakness if we struggle when we have position or responsibility taken away from us or are given a mentor or leader who is "less" in our eyes. When we are not held up for our achievements and works, it may expose a discontented and entitled attitude. We must never forget what we have been graciously given – the undeserved gift of Heaven. Our greatest achievement in life will truly be dying saved.

> *However, do not rejoice that the spirits submit to you, but rejoice that your names are written in Heaven.* (Luke 10:20)

I am so proud of one Christian and dear friend here in Sydney – Lenox Tweneboa. He was a professional soccer player who earned considerable sums of money in his profession around the world. After a year as a Christian in Sydney, he was offered a very attractive contract in Dubai. He would be looked after in royal fashion and have the adulation of new fans and peers. Yet Lennox knew that where he was going did not have a true church of disciples at that time. Therefore, if he had made the decision to go, it would be based on his desires not his spiritual needs. It was so great to see God honor Lennox after he turned down the offer, as only a few months later he baptized his sister into Christ in Sydney and has married the love of his life – our sister Keira.

Conclusion

We must all constantly reflect on how greed can deceive us and remember...

1. How God views greed and embrace that view.
2. To be convinced about how badly it damages us as well as those around us.
3. To constantly recognize what greed is as defined by God's Word not the world.

Then we will struggle so much less with giving money, be more effective in saving others, and build a better relationship with God and with His family.

The challenge is to live simply so that others can simply live.

SECTION TWO

HOW MUCH SHOULD I GIVE?

Chapter 4
Why, How And To Whom We Give

Introduction

The world is full of mistrust when it comes to money and especially when it comes to giving money to churches. Due to the hypocrisy of false ministers taking money to increase their own personal wealth or building expensive venues rather than using it to help people, there is an even greater need to explain to people where all the money they give goes. When people start to understand where all the given money goes, it frees up their hearts to trust, to want to give, and to be proud to give. I am proud to be in a church that has yearly financial presentations to the congregation of how much money is given and where it all goes. It is no wonder that this same church gives generously and sacrificially with a willing heart.

Point I: Why Do We Give?

Why do we give money in the first place? Should not Christianity just be free? That may seem great, however, caring for and looking after people's spiritual health is not cheap.

A. Practicals

We all want to help build God's church, but this costs money. Most of us understand this practice but would be surprised by what expenses come up. So here is a list of just some of the things money goes towards: The hire of venues for church services and other church events such as teen and marrieds events; song books or song sheets; communion trays; flying in guest speakers; pulpits; music stands; audio equipment; church bulletins; food for events; presents and awards for Christians; supplies for children's classes; subsidizing church events such a picnics or retreats; making videos; websites;

telephone bills; computers; benevolence issues; international visas; the cost of moving staff and Christians to churches or mission teams; set up of mission teams; medical care and emergencies; insurances and housing; and of course, the salaries of ministers, women's ministry leaders, interns and in larger congregations, administrators. This list can be endless depending on the wealth of the church members. Usually the poorer the church the greater the needs, as some of our poorer brothers and sisters do not have the money from time to time for even the basics. Consequently, the wealthier churches need to send money to poorer churches just like they did in the early church. (2 Corinthians 8:1-5, 13-15)

B. Benevolence

If any woman who is a believer has widows in her care, she should continue to help them and not let the church be burdened with them, so that the church can help those widows who are really in need. (1 Timothy 5:16)

In most churches, there are separate benevolence contributions given specifically to meet the needs of those Christians who fall on hard times. In many cases, this money that is collected is not enough to cover the needs, so money from our regular contribution is used as well. Over the years, I have found that giving to the benevolence contribution is often an afterthought for most Christians. Many just put in what they find in their pockets that day or evening. Yet when a Christian genuinely needs help they have an expectation that their needs be met with more attention than an afterthought. If this describes you, then I would encourage you to set aside a weekly amount that you have prayed and agreed about between you and God that you will dedicate to giving specifically for the needs of the poor in God's church.

C. To Have Full-Time Staff

> *He ordered the people living in Jerusalem to give the portion due the priests and Levites so they could devote themselves to the Law of the Lord.* (2 Chronicles 31:4)

> *Do you not know that those who serve in the Temple get their food from the Temple, and that those who serve at the altar share in what is offered on the altar? In the same way, the Lord has commanded that those who preach the Gospel should receive their living from the Gospel.*
> (1 Corinthians 9:13-14)

There should be no difference in the commitment level to love God, His people and His mission between those paid full-time to do the work of the ministry and those not employed. We are all called to love the Lord with everything we have and to give up everything. Yet there is a need to have people devoted to training and being trained in how to do the ministry.

We need to free up men and women to be trained in the ministry, then they can become full of Biblical knowledge and develop ministry skills, so they can be effective for God. We also need to support those that have learned to be effective in the ministry. As the church grows, there is also a need for full-time accountants, administrators and many more roles to oversee the good works God has prepared for us in advance to do. (Ephesians 2:10) There is nearly always a direct correlation between the health and growth of a church and the skill and number of full-time leaders in a church. (Matthew 9:37)

Point II: The Church Gives As A Family Not As A Business

A. The Early Church Was A Needs Based Church

All the believers were together and had everything in common. They sold property and possessions to give to anyone who had need. (Acts 2:44-45)

All the believers were one in heart and mind. No one claimed that any of their possessions was their own, but they shared everything they had. With great power the Apostles continued to testify to the resurrection of the Lord Jesus. And God's grace was so powerfully at work in them all that there were no needy persons among them. For from time to time those who owned land or houses sold them, brought the money from the sales and put it at the Apostles' feet, and it was distributed to anyone who had need. Joseph, a Levite from Cyprus, whom the Apostles called Barnabas (which means "son of encouragement"), sold a field he owned and brought the money and put it at the Apostles' feet. (Acts 4:32-37)

Share with the Lord's people who are in need. Practice hospitality. (Romans 12:13)

Do everything you can to help Zenas the Lawyer and Apollos on their way and see that they have everything they need. (Titus 3:13)

Anyone who has been stealing must steal no longer, but must work, doing something useful with their own hands, that they may have something to share with those in need. (Ephesians 4:28)

The early church had many needs as does any growing church — some foreseen, some unforeseen. In the Scriptures concerning the early church, there was no mention of using the Jewish system of giving, no Temple money box, no tithing. They simply had needs as a church, and as a church they worked together to meet those needs. God expects us to look after the needs of all and any brother or sister throughout His worldwide Kingdom.

> *This is how we know what love is: Jesus Christ laid down His life for us. And we ought to lay down our lives for our brothers. If anyone has material possessions and sees his brother in need but has no pity on him, how can the love of God be in him?* (1 John 3:16-17)

B. The Challenge With Being Needs Based

The challenge for most people in working within a "needs based structure of giving" is that it constantly changes, and most people dislike constant change. We like budgets and knowing what is going to be asked of us, so we can plan. This is called living by sight (that's how non-Christians live), yet God wants us to live by faith, to depend and rely on Him so that our faith increases. It reminds us that we serve a God who truly loves us. This is demonstrated by Him providing and rescuing us repeatedly.

> *For we live by faith, not by sight.* (2 Corinthians 5:7)

As with the nation of Israel in the desert, we as God's spiritual Israel must learn to rely on God for our needs to be met. God wants a people who do not rely on themselves and become proud, but a people who need and want to rely on Him daily. He will create and allow needs in His church to humble us, to make us turn toward Him, so He can demonstrate His power to us.

> *He humbled you, causing you to hunger and then feeding you with manna, which neither you nor your ancestors had known, to teach you that man does not live on bread alone but on every word that comes from the mouth of the Lord.*

Your clothes did not wear out and your feet did not swell during these forty years. (Deuteronomy 8:3-4)

God determines the needs of the church; it is His Kingdom not ours. The Kingdom's or church's budget – be it $1,000 per week or $100,000 per week as well as money raised for missions and other plans of God – are determined by many factors. Two critical issues are how many Christians God converts and who He has called to be missionaries. Since God causes His church to grow (Colossians 2:19), He creates new opportunities for the Gospel to be preached as a movement that are not in our plans, but He expects us to respond to the call. (Acts 16:6-10) Other financial needs arise as God allows young and old ministers to "fail forward." These include, laws changing that we cannot foresee, Satan's schemes and other trials that God sends or allows to happen. Life always has more challenges than we expect or want, as an individual, as a church and as a movement. As mentioned before, being asked to give to meet these escalating financial needs does not make us struggle in and of themselves; they merely show if we are struggling in our faith or discipline. God is still sovereign, and He will always come through for us.

And my God will meet all your needs according to the riches of His glory in Christ Jesus. (Philippians 4:19)

C. A Brotherhood Of Needs

When God looks down on the earth, He does not just see you and your church as His church, but all of His children in all of His churches worldwide. He considers us a brotherhood of believers that are to be perfectly unified in mind, heart, doctrine and financially with no divisions. (1 Corinthians 1:10) The challenges of our brothers in the third world churches are just as much a need to be met as the needs in your local church. The answer to the question, *"Am I my brother's keeper?"* even though you do not know "them" is "YES!" (John 13:34-35).

> *Our desire is not that others might be relieved while you are hard pressed, but that there might be equality. At the present time your plenty will supply what they need, so that in turn their plenty will supply what you need. The goal is equality.* (2 Corinthians 8:13-14)

This will always lead to a higher demand for money from the first and second world Christians to provide and give to those less fortunate in the third world. This may in turn lead to feelings of being pressurized or demanded of more than a person or church would like. What we must keep in mind is that we are fortunate to be in a situation where money is much easier to come by than in the third world. This is also true when it comes to sending out missionaries and mission teams. Some may sadly see the churches in the third world as a bottomless hole of needs. This was true when the Apostle Paul set up churches:

> *Moreover, as you Philippians know, in the early days of your acquaintance with the Gospel, when I set out from Macedonia, not one church shared with me in the matter of giving and receiving, except you only; for even when I was in Thessalonica, you sent me aid more than once when I was in need.* (Philippians 4:15-16)

We again need to be thankful that in the past a missionary was sent to set up a church where we were living so that we could be saved. The only option to not living a life where we are constantly sacrificing and giving of ourselves to save those less fortunate, is to become a person or church that is unconcerned about the plight of the world, and God has very strong feelings towards being unconcerned.

> *Now this was the sin of your sister Sodom: She and her*

daughters were arrogant, overfed and unconcerned; they did not help the poor and needy. They were haughty and did detestable things before me. Therefore I did away with them as you have seen. (Ezekiel 16:49-50)

Point III: How Much Should I Give And How?

A. Well How Much Do You Have?

Jesus had no problem in calling people to give up their jobs and careers or their wealth (Mark 10:21), not one reservation about it. When He saw the widow give up all she had, He did not run after her to tell her to not be so stupid, or to be reasonable and just give one of the two coins. You cannot out give God with anything you give Him for the sake of the Kingdom; He promises He will give you back much, much more.

> *"Truly I tell you," Jesus said to them, "no one who has left home or wife or brothers or sisters or parents or children for the sake of the Kingdom of God will fail to receive many times as much in this age, and in the age to come eternal life.* (Luke 18:29-30)

If we start our giving from the point that God asks us to give up everything when we became Christians (Luke 14:33; Matthew 13:44-46), then we will not struggle in giving large amounts of our wealth to God to be used to advance His Kingdom. Yet if we hold on to our money as if it belongs to us, then giving will always be an issue over which we will struggle, no matter how big or small the call to give may be.

Trouble may enter our hearts when we compare ourselves to other Christians and what they give, as opposed to comparing ourselves to Christ and the fact that He gave up everything for us. We are called to be rich towards God (Luke 12:21) not rich towards ourselves. It is said that a good man asks, "why?" While a godly man asks, "why not?" Why not give all? Why not give most of my wealth instead of what seems reasonable or a percentage? If God is God, if He is all powerful and generous, then you simply cannot out give Him. Why not give and give and give? Jesus did!

One of the early converts in Sydney came to us after wanting to leave His church because he had been studying out tithing in the Old Testament. He concluded that his church was wrong in insisting that he only tithe, which is the Old Covenant standard. This led to us getting together and doing a series of studies about what the Bible taught and the standard of the New Covenant. He became a Christian a month later and when we studied out contribution in the Bible, he decided to give a generous amount to God. One of the comments that I remember us laughing about was when his old church insisted on applying the tithing system to his giving, that he was reluctant about giving that amount. Yet as a sold-out disciple, he gave far beyond ten percent of his income because he now wanted to as he understood the heart of God much better.

B. How Much Is Too Much?

> *And now, brothers and sisters, we want you to know about the grace that God has given the Macedonian Churches. In the midst of a very severe trial, their overflowing joy and their extreme poverty welled up in rich generosity. For I testify that they gave as much as they were able, and even beyond their ability. Entirely on their own, they urgently pleaded with us for the privilege of sharing in this service to the Lord's people.* (2 Corinthians 8:1-4)

The Macedonian Christians were in extreme poverty and undergoing a severe trial. Yet they were generous beyond their ability to give.

What does that mean? Did they willingly fast for days or weeks, to give the money they would have spent on food to the needs of furthering the gospel in some foreign land? Did they sell essentials with the faith that God would provide? Did they sell houses to then live in rented accommodation for the rest of their lives? We will never know. The issue was never how much was too much for them to give, but the real issue lies with how much is too much for you? What are the limits of your giving and why?

In a case of giving that Jesus held up in front of the disciples, the widow giving two coins (Luke 21:4), He made mention that she gave out of her poverty not her wealth. If fact, Jesus said that she sacrificed all she had. When we are in Heaven, will we regret that we could have died with more savings in the bank? Will we regret that our retirement could have been more comfortable? Will we regret that our children could have had a better education? Or will we regret that we did not save more people, more family and more friends if we had given more money? Maybe these Christians in the Macedonian Churches had a better grasp of the eternal good of their sacrifices than we do with our giving. Their example is an upward call to us when we think we are asked to give too much for the sake of God's Kingdom.

C. Practicals Of Giving

Now about the collection for God's people: Do what I told the Galatian Churches to do. On the first day of every week, each one of you should set aside a sum of money in keeping with his income, saving it up, so that when I come no collections will have to be made. Then, when I arrive, I will give letters of introduction to the men you approve and send them with your gift to Jerusalem. If it seems advisable for me to go also, they will accompany me.
(1 Corinthians 16:1-4)

Over spending, losing money, mismanagement of money and the temptation to pay the worldly bills before the spiritual ones, are all struggles for most of us at some point in our lives. So how do we make good spiritual decisions with our wealth? How do we make sure that we honor God with the firstfruits of our wealth? (Proverbs 3:9-10)

Give as soon as you get paid, so you cannot over spend. If you get paid weekly or monthly, give to God as soon as you get it, then you cannot give it somewhere else. That is why in the Old Testament God asks for the firstfruits! If you can, do it straight from your bank account so it automatically comes out. If you can't do that, put it in an envelope and set it aside or give it to someone so you cannot spend it. This was the sort of instruction Paul was giving here to the church in Corinth as well as the churches in Galatia.

I have over heard someone even recommend to one of my friends not to give their contribution, because they could not pay their rent if they did. This advice seems in the world's eyes to be logical. Yet by doing so, you are placing more importance on meeting your worldly obligations than your spiritual ones, putting the importance of pleasing your landlord above the importance of pleasing God. In addressing this same issue in the Book of Malachi, God says:

> **"A son honors his father, and a slave his master. If I am a father, where is the honor due me? If I am a master, where is the respect due me?" says the Lord Almighty.**
> (Malachi 1:6)

I am proud to say that my friend gave first to God and then watched God take care of his rent!

Conclusion

When we Understand:

1. Why we give.
2. How we give, as a family meeting the global needs of God's movement.
3. Then we can give regularly, unsparingly and willingly as God desires.

   Each man should give what he has decided in his heart to give, not reluctantly or under compulsion, for God loves a cheerful giver. (2 Corinthians 9:7)

Chapter 5
A Call To Generosity Not Tithing

Introduction

Many people that have been brought up in churches today are taught that tithing is what Christians are commanded to do. What is generally meant by this is that one gives a tenth of their income to God through the church to be used for paying the ministry staff and expenses of the church. Most are called to give 10% before taxes and other deductions are taken out of their pay check; others are called to give 10% after those things are taken out.

Many people believe this is what the Christians in the early church did and therefore this is what we should do. It would surprise most to learn that there is no record of the early Christians in the Bible doing this or being taught to do this. This teaching or understanding of tithing is not even in the Old Testament. Few know that the concept of giving a tenth of your income in the church was something brought into Christendom by the Catholic Church. In 585 AD at the Synod (Council) of Mâçon, they embedded the practice into Church Canon Law. This was the same Synod that brought in other laws such as banning Jews from walking on the public streets at certain times. A millennium later, the Catholic Church at the Council of Trent passed the law that it would excommunicate you if as a Catholic you declined to contribute your tithe.

Many of our childhood beliefs are brought into question as we study the Bible. We often find that they are based more on church tradition rather than on sound Biblical truth. Commanding Christians to give 10% of what they earn is not a command found in the Bible under the New Covenant.

So, let's examine what the Bible does say on this topic.

Point I: What Was Tithing, And Does It Apply to Us Today?

A. What Was Tithing As Described In The Old Testament?

The tithing system described in the Bible in the Old Testament was designed specifically to meet the needs of the religious, economic and political system of the ancient country of Israel. Each of the twelve tribes of Israel, except the tribe of Levi, initially received an allotment of land in the Promised Land of Canaan. The Levites were assistants to Israel's priests and were supported from a tithe offering from other eleven tribes. All families of those eleven tribes were to set aside a tenth of all produce, flocks and cattle from which the Levites would be supported. In turn, the Levites were to give a tenth of that to support the priests. (Leviticus 27:30-33; Numbers 18:21-28) Yet the tithes were not solely to be given to the Levites. The tithes were also used to meet the needs of foreigners, orphans and widows.

> *When you have finished setting aside a tenth of all your produce in the third year, the year of the tithe, you shall give it to the Levite, the foreigner, the fatherless and the widow, so that they may eat in your towns and be satisfied. Then say to the Lord your God: "I have removed from my house the sacred portion and have given it to the Levite, the foreigner, the fatherless and the widow, according to all you commanded. I have not turned aside from your commands nor have I forgotten any of them.*
> (Deuteronomy 26:12-13)

In Deuteronomy 12, God gives clear direction that every person was to take a tithe of their produce and go before God to a place of His choosing (this was later to be at the Temple). After giving the priests their share, the people would eat the remainder themselves in celebration before God. Only on the third year was all the yearly tithe to be given to support the Levites, the foreigners, fatherless and widows by storing it in the towns for distribution over the following three years.

> *Be sure to set aside a tenth of all that your fields produce each year. Eat the tithe of your grain, new wine and olive oil, and the firstborn of your herds and flocks in the presence of the Lord your God at the place He will choose as a dwelling for His Name, so that you may learn to revere the Lord your God always. But if that place is too distant and you have been blessed by the Lord your God and cannot carry your tithe (because the place where the Lord will choose to put His Name is so far away), then exchange your tithe for silver, and take the silver with you and go to the place the Lord your God will choose. Use the silver to buy whatever you like: cattle, sheep, wine or other fermented drink, or anything you wish. Then you and your household shall eat there in the presence of the Lord your God and rejoice. And do not neglect the Levites living in your towns, for they have no allotment or inheritance of their own.*
>
> *At the end of every three years, bring all the tithes of that year's produce and store it in your towns, so that the Levites (who have no allotment or inheritance of their own) and the foreigners, the fatherless and the widows who live in your towns may come and eat and be satisfied, and so that the Lord your God may bless you in all the work of your hands.* (Deuteronomy 14:22-29)

So, if a church was to implement or command tithing based on these Old Covenant principles today, the equivalent might look like commanding all the members to save up 10% of their income to go on a big family holiday together with other Christians and ministers to celebrate before God every year, except the third year they would forgo their holiday and give that year's tithe to the church to provide for the ministers, the foreigners, fatherless and widows. Besides this, if a church were to justify this command by using or referring to the Old Covenant laws they would also be required to implement or command the other laws under the Old Covenant such as celebrating festivals every year (Exodus 23:14-19; Deuteronomy 16:16-17), redeeming of all our firstborn (Exodus 34:19-20), make restitution for wrongs (Numbers 5:5-10), giving freewill offerings and fulfilment of vows (Leviticus 22:21), as well as to make sin offerings, guilt offerings, etc.

B. What Are The Negative Effects Of Teaching Tithing Today?

Giving a tithe did not guarantee righteousness even under the Old Covenant. Even those who did give a tithe legalistically like the Pharisees were still greedy and self-indulgent.

> *Woe to you, teachers of the Law and Pharisees, you hypocrites! You give a tenth of your spices, mint, dill and cumin. But you have neglected the more important matters of the Law – justice, mercy and faithfulness. You should have practiced the latter, without neglecting the former. You blind guides! You strain out a gnat but swallow a camel. Woe to you, teachers of the Law and Pharisees, you hypocrites! You clean the outside of the cup and dish, but inside they are full of greed and self-indulgence.* (Matthew 23:23-25)

If you were to continually use giving a tenth of your income as a rule of thumb for what you give, or a group gives, it can lead to greed on the part of the rich for whom giving a tenth of their income is neither generous or sacrificial (as with the teachers of the Law and Pharisees), also oppression on the part of the poor for whom it could be too much. Consider a widow with three children under ten years old, who is uneducated and works by selling food she makes on the side of the road. She has no savings and rents a house. If she were to give a tenth of her income, it would be a great sacrifice for her as her needs versus her income are great. It would most likely be a sacrifice that would be unachievable.

We cannot refer to Old Covenant Scriptures such as Malachi 3:10 that command all to give their tithe regardless of their situation and apply it to the poor in the global church today, commanding them to also give a tithe. There was a system in the nation of Israel, created by God, to care and feed the poor and widows that does not exist in some countries today. Farmers would only reap their harvest once leaving food for the poor to gather up (glean) as seen in the case of Ruth. (Ruth 2:2; also see Exodus 23:10- 11; Leviticus 19:10; Deuteronomy 15:1-11) God also commanded that the national tithe given in the third year was to be used for the poor widows, orphans and foreigners in need.

Compare this to a young man who works hard, is educated, and as a student gives a tenth of what he earns, say $10 per week. Then he graduates, gets a job and continues to give a tenth of what he has all his life. His salary raises from $100 per week, to $200, then $500, then $1,000, then $2,000. As his wealth increases so does his appetite for things. He buys a car, a house, clothes and finds more expensive places to eat. He now earns $100,000 a year. Yes, he has more things to pay for, more commitments, yet he still gives a tenth of his wage. Is giving $10,000 a year out of $100,000 greedy? I am sure if you asked this man when he was a student this question he would have said yes, or something like, "If I ever get to earn $100,000 a year (about $2,000 per week) there is no way I would only give tenth to God. That would only be $200 a week. What would I need the other $1,800 per week for unless I had become materialistic?"

At the beginning of the church planting in Sydney, we were blessed after a few months to have a young married couple join us with their two children – Joe & Chesca Ugorgi. More than any couple that I have met, Joe & Chesca embodied the example of giving generously as opposed to merely giving 10% of their wealth. Joe was converted as a teen; did well as a Christian when he was a student; later studied as a doctor; and then graduated in the field of Diagnostic Radiology. He went from a student salary to a white-collar professional salary. Yet all the time in Sydney when his salary jumped to over $200,000 USD, he rented a menial house and secured most of his furniture second hand or free. He then opened his home for two Christians to live for free and gave $1,000 a week in contribution! Moreover, he gave much more of his wealth for missions! Instead of increasing his standard of living, he increased his standard of giving. Joe and his family had a wealthy income yet lived simply to financially fuel our fledgling church.

My point is not that the poor should not give to God at all, but that those with wealth should not oppress the poor or justify themselves before God as righteous just because they give a 10% of their income which really is not a challenge or sacrifice for them. (Luke 18:9-12)

C. Tithing Was An Old Covenant Law So We Are Free From It As A Christian

Tithing was an Old Covenant Law given to the nation of Israel, which Jesus took away by nailing it to the cross. We are now under a New Covenant:

When you were dead in your sins and in the uncircumcision of your sinful nature, God made you alive with Christ. He forgave us all our sins, having canceled the written code, with its regulations, that was against us and that stood opposed to us; He took it away, nailing it to the cross. (Colossians 2:13-14)

These are a shadow of the things that were to come; the reality, however, is found in Christ. (Colossians 2:17)

This verse teaches that the Law was only a shadow of the reality; the reality is found in Christ. Yes, there are parallels between the Old Covenant features and the New Covenant realities, but the two covenants are distinct. Today the Old Covenant is obsolete:

By calling this covenant "new," He has made the first one obsolete; and what is obsolete and aging will soon disappear. (Hebrews 8:13)

There are a few references to tithing in the New Testament (Matthew 23:23; Luke 11:42, 18:12; Hebrews 7:5-9), but all refer to the Old Covenant system which was still in effect during Jesus' ministry. Significant is the fact that the Book of Acts – which records the first 30 years of the church – has no mention of tithing or teaching of tithing. In the very early church the Christians were from a Jewish background and may well have given as they had when they were Jews, only now instead of giving at the temple and to the Levites, they gave to the Apostles who would then distributed the wealth to meet the needs of the early church. (Acts 4:32-35) Some Jewish Christians tried to wrongly enforce all Christians to obey the Old Covenant Law (Acts 15:5), yet there was no directive for anyone in the early church to tithe or to teach tithing to Christians from a Gentile background. (Acts 15:29) Jesus does not teach that we are to obey according to the Law of the Old Covenant found in the Old Testament, but to go beyond the Law in everything as seen in His teaching in the Sermon on the Mount in Matthew 5, 6 and 7. This same principle is applied in what we must give up; it is not simply a percentage of our lives but everything:

> *In the same way, those of you who do not give up everything you have cannot be my disciples.*
> (Luke 14:33)

Point II: A Call To Generosity

God is generous! He richly provides us with everything we need. (1 Timothy 6:17) He gives generously. (James 1:5) In the parable of the Workers of the Vineyard, the landowner who represents God says, *"'Or are you envious because I am generous?' So the last will be first, and the first will be last."* (Matthew 20:15b-16) It is God's nature to be generous in all things. He does not treat us as our sins deserve. (Psalm 103:10) The extent of His love is like no other. (John 3:16; Titus 3:5-7) Even the concept of grace is generous. Therefore, if we are to be godly, to be like God, then we too are to be generous!

A. Generosity Is An Attitude

> *And now, brothers, we want you to know about the grace that God has given the Macedonian Churches. Out of the most severe trial, their overflowing joy and their extreme poverty welled up in rich generosity. For I testify that they gave as much as they were able, and even beyond their ability. Entirely on their own, they urgently pleaded with us for the privilege of sharing in this service to the saints. And they did not do as we expected, but*

they gave themselves first to the Lord and then to us in keeping with God's will. So we urged Titus, since he had earlier made a beginning, to bring also to completion this act of grace on your part. But just as you excel in everything, in faith, in speech, in knowledge, in complete earnestness and in your love for us, see that you also excel in this grace of giving. (2 Corinthians 8:1-7)

According to the *Essential Dictionary,* to be generous is to be "liberally giving, having a readiness to give, freedom from meanness and smallness of mind or character, and to give largely from what you have to amply supply others." The Christians in the early Macedonian Churches set us all a great example. Theirs is an overflowing joy in the privilege of providing for the needs of others despite their challenging situation. They pleaded for the chance to give. How many today have that type of heart, begging, pleading to give individually or as a group?

Most of us like to excel in things in which we are good. For example, if we have a good voice, we like to sing. If we are good cooks, we like to cook for others. In 2 Corinthians 8, God commanded the Corinthian Church to "add" excelling in the grace of giving to the things in which they excelled at. We too need to add to that which we are excellent in by *"[excelling] in the grace of giving."* This is not an option. Just like loving one another is not an option for followers of Christ, we need to *"see that"* we excel in our giving.

At conversion some are encouraged to start their giving at a tenth of their income as a guideline because they have no past reference point for giving. Jacob, the father of the nation of Israel made this self-imposed vow to God after entrusting his life to Him before the Law. (Genesis 28:20-22) Yet continuing to hang on to a strict mentality of giving a tenth of our income to fulfill our righteousness before God, can seriously restrict one's heart from truly being generous towards God. It can make us falsely believe that we are being generous because we compare our giving to the standard of 10% of our wealth as it increases. We do not do this in any other area of our lives. When it comes to the ones we love we do not give just 10% of our time, money or love and consider ourselves justified. We do not time the hours of giving to our spouses or children and consider our duty done. Rather we lavish our love on them. We generously provide for them because we love them. It should be with the same heart that we give to God and His other children in His household.

When I think of giving generously I always think of when I give Christmas presents. I want to encourage and love as many people as possible, yet often finances are limited. (The following is a personal confession!) So, I look at my friends and categories them. I cannot afford to buy everyone a big present, so I base my giving on the closeness and meaningfulness of my relationship with each of them. For some, I write a card with carefully chosen words. For others, I buy them a small present like chocolates. However, for my longtime friends, I want to buy something unique or funny, so I look for it throughout the year and have a certain budget that I allow myself to spend.

When it comes to my dear wife and amazing kids, I have a very different attitude. I do not put a limit on their present. My starting point begins at what they want, and then I try my best to figure out how I can possibly get that present. Why? Because they are my most precious relationships. With them my standard is lavish generosity. So, it should be with all of us with God. As our primary relationship and the love of our lives, there should not be a category in which He resides. Contribution should not be categorized in your budget against bills and food allowances. You must start from the point of what can you give to the love of your life to make Him feel special, lavishing a generous portion of love on Him, and the thing He values most on earth – His Kingdom.

B. Generosity As A Spiritual Law

The world says, "Spend money on yourself and those you love. Occasionally give to those in need." However, most people are not generous unless they see a benefit to themselves or are moved by guilt. It is not a lifestyle. The resistance towards being generous is often the fear of not having enough for yourself later. Yet this is not true when it comes to the spiritual or righteous.

> *I was young and now I am old, yet I have never seen the righteous forsaken or their children begging bread. They are always generous and lend freely; their children will be a blessing.* (Psalms 37:25-26)

> *Good will come to him who is generous and lends freely, who conducts his affairs with justice.* (Psalm 112:5)

> *The generous will themselves be blessed, for they share their food with the poor.* (Proverbs 22:9)

> *One man gives freely, yet gains even more; another withholds unduly, but comes to poverty. A generous man will prosper; he who refreshes others will himself be refreshed.* (Proverbs 22:24-25)

> *The wicked borrow and do not repay, but the righteous give generously.* (Psalms 37:21)

> *A stingy man is eager to get rich and is unaware that poverty awaits him.* (Proverbs 28:22)

Like a physical law – if you eat less food than you need, you lose weight, and if you eat more food than you need, you put on weight – there is a spiritual law at work when it comes to generosity. The more generous you are, the more you prosper and are given. The less generous you are then the less prosperous you become. God has set up the universe to work that way!

C. You Have To Be Generous To Be Given To Generously

Remember this: Whoever sows sparingly will also reap sparingly, and whoever sows generously will also reap generously. Each man should give what he has decided in his heart to give, not reluctantly or under compulsion, for God loves a cheerful giver. And God is able to make all grace abound to you, so that in all things at all times, having all that you need, you will abound in every good work. As it is written: "He has scattered abroad His gifts to the poor; His righteousness endures forever."

Now He who supplies seed to the sower and bread for food will also supply and increase your store of seed and will enlarge the harvest of your righteousness. You will be made rich in every way so that you can be generous on every occasion, and through us your generosity will result in thanksgiving to God. (2 Corinthians 9:6-11)

Again, let me reiterate: Our God is a generous God! He scatters gifts to the poor. He supplies the raw materials (seeds) for people to prosper. He is the one who enlarges harvests. It is He who gives people wealth so that they can be generous. If you are not a generous person, why would He give you wealth if you are only going to be selfish with it? You must first be generous to then be trusted with wealth from God.

The analogy is simple in verse six: *"If you sow sparingly you will reap sparingly."* If you plant a field with 500 seeds of crop, you will get at most 500 shoots or stems of whatever harvest you planted. However, if you plant 1,000 seeds of crop on the land, your harvest will be greater. It is all so logical to a farmer, to God and to a generous man. If you want a bigger crop you sow more. Yet to he who is greedy, fearful or has little to no faith, the temptation is to hold onto the seed you have, to provide for your immediate needs instead of looking to the future. Therefore, providing little for the future. Being "stingy" for any reason only hurts you and prevents you from being made rich in every way.

Point III: Defining Generosity

A. Defined By What You Have Left Over Not By What You Give

> *Jesus sat down opposite the place where the offerings were put and watched the crowd putting their money into the Temple treasury. Many rich people threw in large amounts. But a poor widow came and put in two very small copper coins, worth only a fraction of a penny. Calling His disciples to Him, Jesus said, "I tell you the truth, this poor widow has put more into the treasury than all the others. They all gave out of their wealth; but she, out of her poverty, put in everything – all she had to live on.* (Mark 12:41-44)

Wealthy people can "seem" generous because they give a lot. However, judging the poor on how little they give, does not mean they are not generous. Jesus brings this to the attention of the disciples and therefore we should take note too. Someone who can easily afford to give is not necessarily being generous as they have much left over even after they have given considerable amounts. Generosity is measured by what you have after you give rather than by the amount you give.

B. You Define God's Generosity To You

Give, and it will be given to you. A good measure, pressed down, shaken together and running over, will be poured into your lap. For with the measure you use, it will be measured to you. (Luke 6:38)

Do you define what your generosity is by percentage? Or perhaps only when God seems generous to you, are you then generous with others? For example, when you get a pay raise that you were not expecting or needing, do you give a percentage and then increase your standard of living by spending more or do you give all your increase or most of it to God? Like a father giving a bag of sweets to his child in a social setting, then looking to see if his child will share them with everyone or not. God looks at us to see what we do with our wealth. If we are like a child that does not share the gift from his father, our Father in Heaven will not give us more bags of sweets. Instead He will give the other sweets to everyone but the selfish child. Unless we give the sweets away, we do not put ourselves in the position for God to give us more sweets! We are to become a continual vessel for giving, not the end point of God's generosity.

When God increases your income, increase your giving not your standard of living.

C. Commanding The Rich To Give Generously

Command those who are rich in this present world not to be arrogant nor to put their hope in wealth, which is so uncertain, but to put their hope in God, who richly provides us with everything for our enjoyment.

Command them to do good, to be rich in good deeds, and to be generous and willing to share. (1 Timothy 6:17-18)

Wealth is deceitful (Mark 4:19; Ecclesiastes 5:10), and many who are rich do not see themselves as rich or "ungenerous." This might come from comparing themselves to others in their social settings or looking at their income compared to the expenses they manage, even though many of these expenses are unnecessary. The rich often need an external person to challenge them for them "to see the reality of their situation" before God and how they are being ungenerous. In this passage, Paul is teaching the young evangelist to get with the rich and command them to be generous.

Many times, I have seen leaders not wanting to challenge the biggest givers in their congregations to give more. They may give large amounts compared to most, but under closer investigation, they only give out of their wealth. It may be 12 or even 25 percent of their income but compared with the amount of wealth that they could give it is far from generous.

The other situation where leaders have difficulty challenging their members is when people are awarded pay increases and only give a small percentage of the increase back to the Lord. Here is an example of how I handle it. I am always trying to help my friends in the church to better their careers, and I was working with one friend to get a better job. He was giving somewhat generously from his present income. He was a young Christian from a religious background and was brought up in that church with the misunderstanding to only give a tithe. Indeed, he was now giving beyond that which was a great victory in his growth. Together with God, he secured a new job with a considerable increase, nearly double his income. This was great news, more than he expected. He was also soon to get married, so this was brilliant. Yet when his new income came in, he only increased his contribution by *"some"* (like Cain), but not by double or more. Yes, his giving was more than he was giving before and more than a tithe, but not generous. I asked him about this and he explained that he was worried about the expense of his upcoming wedding. I challenged him that if I had asked him two months before he had the increase, would he have felt great about doubling his contribution if God was to almost double his wage. He said he would have. I then challenged him if he thought he was being generous towards God. I did not want him to answer me but to go and pray to his God that night and talk it through with Him. He did so willingly and that night he adjusted his giving to God to a generous amount. The very next day he was given another undeserved blessing by God in the form of the house that he had wanted to move into with his new wife, from which he had previously been refused. God rewarded his generosity with generosity. He grew in his faith, his giving, his relationship with God, and had a great wedding!

Conclusion

Giving is to be done cheerfully, rather than as an obligation (2 Corinthians 9:6-7) and certainly not for public recognition. (Matthew 6:1-4) The right amount to give may be more or may be less than ten percent, depending on one's circumstances. (Matthew 19:21; Luke 18:22, 21:1-4; Hebrews 13:16; 1 John 3:17) Generous giving is an acknowledgment that everything we have is a gift from God and is to be used in His service. (Luke 12:33; Acts 20:35; 1 Timothy 6:17-19; James 1:17, 1:27; 1 Peter 4:10)

So how much should I give to God and His Kingdom? Well that is a matter between you and God. He has clearly set out the principles for how He gives, the sort of heart He commends, and how He reacts to different types of giving. Ask yourself: Is my giving generous? Do not ask yourself if it is generous compared to others in the church, but generous compared to God. Are you excelling in your giving? Is your giving increasing in line with all the other spiritual areas of your life – love, prayer life, knowledge? Has your generosity ceased to grow? Before you decide what to give, go and talk this through with God, as He is the one to whom we must give account.

If you are leading a group or a church, I would encourage you to make giving in a generous way to God your standard and the standard of your group or church. When the group that you lead willingly gives with lavished generosity to God, then like my friends the Ugorji's, you will see God lavish His love on them in the form of people becoming Christians, family members being saved, and many other blessings. You will see more of God honoring those who honor Him.

Medically, the Ugorji's were told that they were not able to have children. God knew otherwise! I truly believe that in honoring God, God decided to honor them as they now have three incredibly adorable kids!

We should understand that:

1. Tithing was a Law for the nation of Israel and it does not apply to us today.
2. There is a Biblical call to be generous when giving.
3. Your giving should be unquestionably generous and should be open to being challenged.

When you have decided with God to give generously watch and enjoy God's response.

Chapter 6
Special And One Time Contributions

Introduction

When there is a call for Christians to raise money above their weekly giving to support the running of the church, the questions often asked range from, "Are Christian leaders allowed or should they be allowed to do that?" to "Is it Biblical?" In this chapter, we will study out the Scriptures to see what the Bible says on the subject and look at some practical ways of how to go about raising monies in such cases.

Point I: A Spiritual Culture Of Extra Contributions Among God's People

A. One Time Contributions

Throughout the history of God's Kingdom, there were always times where there were calls to raise significant amounts of wealth to achieve God's will and bring Him glory. This can be seen in such the cases as: the building and dedicating of the Tabernacle in the Books of Exodus and Numbers; the building and rebuilding of the Temple and Jerusalem; and giving to God from windfalls such as plunder.

> *The Lord said to Moses, "Tell the Israelites to bring me an offering. You are to receive the offering for me from each man whose heart prompts him to give. These are the offerings you are to receive from them: gold, silver and bronze; blue, purple and scarlet yarn and fine linen; goat hair; ram skins dyed red and hides of sea cows; acacia wood; olive oil for the light; spices for the anointing oil and for the fragrant incense; and onyx stones and other gems to be mounted on the ephod and breastpiece. "Then have*

them make a sanctuary for me, and I will dwell among them." (Exodus 25:1-8)

In the eighteenth year of Josiah's reign, to purify the land and the Temple, he sent Shaphan son of Azaliah and Maaseiah the ruler of the city, with Joah son of Joahaz, the recorder, to repair the Temple of the Lord his God. They went to Hilkiah the high priest and gave him the money that had been brought into the Temple of God, which the Levites who were the doorkeepers had collected from the people of Manasseh, Ephraim and the entire remnant of Israel and from all the people of Judah and Benjamin and the inhabitants of Jerusalem. Then they entrusted it to the men appointed to supervise the work on the Lord's Temple. These men paid the workers who repaired and restored the Temple. (2 Chronicles 34:8-10)

Also see Numbers 7; Numbers 31:25-54; 2 Kings 12:1-16; 1 Chronicles 22; 2 Chronicles 24:1-16 and 2 Chronicles 29.

B. Ongoing Special And One Time Contributions

There was also a culture in God's Kingdom of constantly bringing to God offerings outside of regular tithing and special needs. These were known as free will offerings, special vows or festival offerings. These were seen as a pleasing aroma to God, something He loved, because they were from the heart and an overflow of a person's relationship with Him.

The Lord said to Moses, "Speak to the Israelites and say to them: 'After you enter the land I am giving you as a home and you present to the Lord offerings made by fire, from the herd or the flock, as an aroma pleasing to the Lord, whether burnt offerings or sacrifices, for special vows or freewill offerings or festival offerings.'" (Numbers 15:1-3)

Also see Leviticus 12:5-8; Numbers 18:8-15; Numbers 28 and 29.

C. This Culture Extended Into The Church

Selling their possessions and goods, they gave to anyone as he had need. (Acts 2:45)

When the church first started in Jerusalem, Jews had come from all around the world. (Acts 2:8-11) They had come to celebrate a festival, Pentecost, and most there had not intended to stay a long time. Yet God had other plans. Three thousand were converted and then there were daily baptisms. (Acts 2:41. 47) Since there was only one church, they had to stay together for a time and grew to 5,000 men. (Acts 4:4) So where did they get the money to support each other while they were away from home, lacking regular jobs and income? As with the Jews who built the Tabernacle and the Temple, the young church did whatever it took to fuel and feed the growing church.

All the believers were one in heart and mind. No one claimed that any of his possessions was his own, but they shared everything they had. With great power the Apostles continued to testify to the resurrection of the Lord Jesus, and much grace was upon them all. There were no needy persons among them. For from time to time those who owned lands or houses sold them, brought the money from the sales and put it at the Apostles' feet, and it was distributed to anyone as he had need. Joseph, a Levite from Cyprus, whom the Apostles called Barnabas (which means Son of Encouragement) sold a field he owned and brought the money and put it at the Apostles' feet. (Acts 4:32-37)

There was constant selling of houses and land, and the young church trusted God's chosen leaders to direct the funds as the needs presented themselves. This was not a "one off" event as it happened from time to time. It was not until Acts 8:1 that the church was scattered and all except the Apostles were sent on their way as missionaries by God with the teaching and example that no Christian counted their money or possessions as their own. They pooled their money and resources to further the Kingdom of God. And when greed did appear, as in the example of Ananias and Sapphira, God dealt with it swiftly. (Acts 5:1-11)

Those inside the church who had wealth helped those who did not, not only in their local church but also in the cities and countries outside of their own. The wealth of the churches in richer countries was used to support the work of the churches in the poorer ones.

> *The disciples, each according to his ability, decided to provide help for the brothers living in Judea. This they did, sending their gift to the elders by Barnabas and Saul.*
> (Acts 11:29-30)

Today God has given what we call the first world countries much wealth. Many who consider themselves poor in the first world – when compared to their brothers and sisters in the third world – are extremely rich by comparison. God simply wants world equality in His church.

> *Our desire is not that others might be relieved while you are hard pressed, but that there might be equality.*
> (2 Corinthians 8:13)

Also see Acts 24:17; Romans 15:25-28; 1 Corinthians 16:1-4; and 2 Corinthians 8:1-14.

Point II: Looking To The World For Help

A. God's Principle Of Giving Money To People To Hand It Over To The Righteous

> *A man can do nothing better than to eat and drink and find satisfaction in his work. This too, I see, is from the hand of God, for without Him, who can eat or find enjoyment? To the man who pleases Him, God gives wisdom, knowledge and happiness, but to the sinner He gives the task of gathering and storing up wealth to hand it over to the one who pleases God. This too is meaningless, a chasing after the wind.* (Ecclesiastes 2:24-26)

> *A good man leaves an inheritance for his children's children, but a sinner's wealth is stored up for the righteous.* (Proverbs 13:22)

One of God's ways to provide for His Kingdom financially is to get non-believers to give and supply their wealth so the righteous can use it. Understanding this principle may even help answer the question, "Why does God bless the unrighteous?" Keep in mind it is God who gives man his wealth and ability to make wealth, not man himself. He can easily take it away and give it to whomever He chooses.

> *The Lord sends poverty and wealth; He humbles and He exalts.* (1 Samuel 2:7)

B. Examples Of This Principle

Plundering the Egyptians: It was always God's plan to numerically grow the nation of Israel from Jacob's small tribe of 70 to be *"as numerous as the stars in the sky."* When they left Egypt, God had a plan to supply the Israelites with the money and materials necessary to finance the Exodus and start of the Kingdom of Israel. He revealed this plan to Abraham in Genesis 15:7-15. We then see this prophecy played out and fulfilled in Exodus 3:21-22; Exodus 11:2-3; and Exodus 12:35-36.

When the Israelites went into the Promised Land, they inhabited a land that God had predestined them to take from others. This *"land of milk and honey"* had been prepared for the Israelites. Those they conquered had previously toiled, managed and made the land good for providing food. God gave them cities, houses and plunder from God's enemies to provide for every need of His people. (Numbers 31:7-12; Deuteronomy 20:10-15; and Joshua 11:14)

The wealth David used to build God's Kingdom and later His Temple came from the plunder that David took from God's enemies. (2 Samuel 8: 7-12; 2 Samuel 12:29-30) Israel's wealth was further increased under King Solomon's reign by those outside of the Kingdom of Israel bringing it freely to Solomon. (2 Chronicles 9:22-24)

It was even prophesied that the rebuilding of Jerusalem and the Temple was to be rebuilt using the wealth and power of those outside God's Kingdom.

> *Foreigners will rebuild your walls, and their kings will serve you.* (Isaiah 60:10)

This is also talked about in Isaiah 23:17-18 and in Isaiah 61:6. The scene is King Cyrus providing provisions for Ezra. This was prophesied in Isaiah 45 then fulfilled in Ezra 1:1-11 and reconfirmed by King Darius in Ezra 6:1-10, 22. Then King Artaxerxes provides wealth for Ezra to go to Jerusalem. (Ezra 7:11-27)

When Jesus was born, God brought wise men from distant lands to provide wealth for Joseph and Mary for their escape into Egypt.

> *On coming to the house, they saw the child with His mother Mary, and they bowed down and worshiped Him. Then they opened their treasures and presented Him with gifts of gold, frankincense and myrrh.* (Matthew 2: 11)

God provided for Jesus during His ministry as He was invited to houses for feasts. He gave Jesus the ability to find money that had been lost by others to use to pay taxes. (Matthew 17:24-27) God even provided Him with means of transport – a donkey. (Matthew 21:1-2)

C. God Expects Us To Act On This Principle

God moves and prepares non-believers' hearts to give money to fuel God's Kingdom. Do you believe that? God wants you to. The only question is, will you act upon it?

The process today is much the same as when the Israelites plundered the Egyptians. Stage one: God's Word promised it would happen. Stage two: God's leader, who at that time was Moses, had to tell the people to do it. Stage three: The people obeyed, and they were given whatever they asked.

> Stage 1: *And I will make the Egyptians favorably disposed toward this people, so that when you leave you will not go empty-handed. Every woman is to ask her neighbor and any woman living in her house for articles of silver and gold and for clothing, which you will put on your sons and daughters. And so you will plunder the Egyptians.* (Exodus 3:21-22)

> Stage 2: *Tell the people that men and women alike are to*

ask their neighbors for articles of silver and gold. (The Lord made the Egyptians favorably disposed toward the people, and Moses himself was highly regarded in Egypt by Pharaoh's officials and by the people.) (Exodus 11:2-3)

Stage 3: *The Israelites did as Moses instructed and asked the Egyptians for articles of silver and gold and for clothing. The Lord had made the Egyptians favorably disposed toward the people, and they gave them what they asked for; so they plundered the Egyptians.* (Exodus 12:35-36)

What is apparent through all of this is that God was working powerfully, *"I will make the Egyptians favorably disposed toward this people"* and *"The Lord made the Egyptians favorably disposed toward the people."*

One of the ways God helps us to believe in Him, is by giving us money that we think is hard or impossible to attain.

> *I will give you the treasures of darkness, riches stored in secret places, so that you may know that I am the Lord, the God of Israel, who summons you by name.* (Isaiah 45:3)

Point III: The Practicals Of Raising Money

There is money to be found everywhere. I was reminded of this last year as I was evangelizing at the beach in Sydney in the evening and I saw a man with a metal detector combing the beach. When I talked to him, he explained that what he was doing was getting all the money, phones and jewelry dropped in the sand every day by people. He collected an average of $70 a day and on occasion had found much larger amounts. The issue is not so much can money be "found" to fuel the evangelization of the world, but how to do it.

A. Money God Gave Us Before We Were Christians

Many people become Christians having spent their life focusing on building their personal wealth and hoarding possessions that they do not need but wanted. Look in your wardrobe, your cupboards, your kitchen; most will find clothes, gadgets and an array of goods that you rarely ever use, things that you once wanted but do not need. When we become Christians, we change the direction of our hearts. We become rich toward God as opposed to rich toward ourselves, as we focus not so much on personal savings for ourselves but saving others. We become sellers of our worldly goods rather than buyers.

> *And I'll say to myself, "You have plenty of grain laid up for many years. Take life easy; eat, drink and be merry." But God said to him, "You fool! This very night your life will be demanded from you. Then who will get what you have prepared for yourself?" This is how it will be with anyone who stores up things for himself but is not rich toward God.* (Luke 12:19-21)

> *Selling their possessions and goods, they gave to anyone as he had need.* (Acts 2:45)

No Christian will die wishing they had more savings left behind in the bank; but when judgement day comes, we will all wish more people were saved through the way that we lived our lives.

B. Using Your Talents

> *The man who had received the five talents brought the other five. "Master," he said, "you entrusted me with five talents. See, I have gained five more."* (Matthew 25:20)

God gave us all talents and expects us to put them to work, some obvious and some hidden. We can apply these to raising money, be it working overtime, hosting bake-off sales, cupcakes sales, busking (performing on the street), buying and reselling Christmas cards, BBQ's, cooking everyone's lunch at work for a week, five aside football tournaments with entry fee, etc. I have found that there are always new ways that others are raising money for numerous charities that I have not considered. By simply using the internet to look up "101 ways to fundraise" or "A - Z of fundraising ideas," you can find countless ideas and inspiring ways.

C. Special Events

Individual Events: These can be a great way to enrich anyone's life. In 2013, I was looking for ways to raise money for church missions, so I scanned the Internet googling, "Most effective personal event to raise money for charity." In that year, it said that the most effective personal fundraising event was a marathon. (People like to sponsor people who are doing something challenging.) The average sponsor would donate $150. I was 46 and had never run more than four miles in my life. But with a few brave friends, we decided to run the Los Angeles Marathon. The event changed my life, health, character and raised thousands of dollars for missions. These events can be highlights of our lives. I have walked 3 1/2 days across Hadrian's Wall in the UK to raise money for missions, as well as many other events. It can be something less demanding, a sponsored head shave or beard shave, a bad tie day at work, getting everyone to donate their unwanted clothes and holding a sale at work or among friends, filling a jar with sweets and getting everyone at work to guess for $5. One of my all-time favorites that I saw when I was a young Christian was two disciples in London making incredible costumes and dressing up as Batman and the Joker, heading to Central London on a Saturday, and asking for donations as people took photos with them!

Group Events: These are especially necessary for those who need the encouragement and have time and ability challenges. They can range from sponsored litter pick-ups, walkathons, car washes, ugly face pulling competitions, and all sorts of novel ideas that the internet expertly lists. One of the important issues in choosing your event is picking the most effective one for your situation, because not everything that works for others will work for you.

When I was leading a church in the UK trying to raise money for missions, the city had so many of its inhabitants who did not believe in God or believed in other faiths. So, we arranged with the local children's hospital to spend the day, cleaning, painting and gardening their grounds and made this a sponsored event. As a result, when we went door to door to raise money clearly stating it was for mission work, I know some people gave not so much because of the cause but because we were doing something in the community that benefited them or might benefit them and their children in the future.

D. Blatant Boldness

> *The wicked man flees though no one pursues, but the righteous are as bold as a lion*. (Proverbs 28:1)

If you are genuinely passionate about a cause – and in the case of Christians, believe God has given money to non-believers for the express reason of handing it over to believers – this will make you bold. You will be amazed at what and who God has prepared to give you funds for His use. One of the ways that I have seen God work is to write letters to companies I did not know but who were owner operated. I asked them directly for money for missions explaining all the good our church does in marriage counselling, helping people get off drugs, mentoring teenagers, helping the elderly, as well as the lonely. I have asked my landlord to donate a month's rent; asked people if they ever have given to charity and then asked them to give their estimated yearly amount to missions at my church. Other ideas that I have used were approaching local companies to donate gifts to be raffled off at a church auction or a special event. I have door knocked all my neighbors to ask them to donate goods for a garage sale that I then hosted, and all the proceeds went to missions. You can just ask people if they think church and mission work is a worthy cause, and if they say yes, ask them for donations. Most people who have wealth and a good life want to help others and give back. Once you explain what we do with the money like healing marriages through counselling, giving free parenting workshops, and supporting students through their university years, many are happy to give.

Conclusion

So, we see from the Scriptures that:

1. God's Kingdom, be it Israel under the Old Covenant or His church under the New Covenant, had a culture of raising funds through extra contributions.
2. God always provides ways for these funds to be found including collecting the wealth of others that God has predestined for us to use.
3. There are many practical ways of raising money. We just need to be bold, creative and to quote Nike, "Just do it!"

> *Therefore, since we have such a hope, we are very bold.*
> (2 Corinthians 3:12)

SECTION THREE

WHY WITHOLD FROM THE GIVER?

Chapter 7
God Gives And Takes Away Wealth For A Reason

Introduction

In the Parable of the Talents in Matthew 25:14-30, we see the master entrusted three servants with wealth. He expected them to use that wealth and it does not say that he gave them specific instructions. It was his assumption that if you were given money you would do something with it. At the end of the story, we see the master giving more to the two who had done something with their money and taking it from the one who did nothing with it. This story was for the chosen Jews, who were given the Promised Land, not because they were righteous or great, but to be righteous with it and do something great with it. They failed at doing that, so God took away salvation from the Jews and gave it to all.

Today God gives us wealth and talents to use for righteousness and to do great spiritual things, otherwise He will take it away.

Point I: God Gives You Wealth

A. God Gives Us Talents That Enable Us To Create Wealth

You must always remember that it is God who gives you your character, talents and knowledge to make you successful. He put your soul into your body with set genes, in a specific family, in a particular country and with the ability to get an education. You could have been born in any family at any time, but He divinely chose the one you have. With this came unique privileges and inherited talents. Not only that, but as Christians we learn so much from the Bible and other Christians that it continually increases our talents. All this comes from God and makes us prosper. We must always remember this and give thanks for it.

> *My son, do not forget my teaching, but keep my commands in your heart, for they will prolong your life many years and bring you prosperity.* (Proverbs 3:1-2)

> *He who pursues righteousness and love finds life, prosperity and honor.* (Proverbs 21:21)

> *Praise the Lord. Blessed is the man who fears the Lord, who finds great delight in His commands. His children will be mighty in the land; the generation of the upright will be blessed. Wealth and riches are in his house, and his righteousness endures forever.* (Psalms 112:1-3)

In my last job before returning to the ministry and the mission field, when I was interviewed, I told my employer that I do not lie. If I were asked to lie, then I would quit my job. The role was in recruitment which has a large sales aspect to it, so most people do not tell "the truth, the whole truth and nothing but the truth." As a State Manager, I would also hire people and when I interviewed them I told them that I never lie, and if they lied, I would fire them. This lost me many potential employees. My boss even challenged me after a year that I was going to have to really prove to him that I could win business by not lying. In the five years that I worked there, I was promoted to National Sales Manager, then to National Operations Manager. I won much repeat business due to my honesty and much new business purely because of that conviction. I would tell clients as a selling point that I could not lie because I was a real Christian. My God gave to me the "talent of not lying" (as I used to lie a lot before I was a Christian), and this propelled by career. It also made people want to work for me and stay working for me.

The greatest compliment that I had because of this, was going to a recruitment networking event and having someone introduce themselves while saying they had heard of me, "the recruiter who never lies." As Solomon said, *"A good name is better than fine perfume."* (Ecclesiastes 7:1)

B. God Controls Who Has And Who Does Not Have Wealth

> *The Lord sends poverty and wealth; He humbles and He exalts. He raises the poor from the dust and lifts the needy from the ash heap; He seats them with princes and has them inherit a throne of honor. "For the foundations of the earth are the Lord's; upon them He has set the world.* (1 Samuel 2:7-8)

> *The blessing of the Lord brings wealth, and He adds no trouble to it.* (Proverbs 10:22)

> *I form the light and create darkness, I bring prosperity and create disaster; I, the Lord, do all these things.* (Isaiah 45:7)

> *He provides food for those who fear Him; He remembers His covenant forever.* (Psalms 111:5)

Beyond our ability given by God to make wealth, He also determines who gets what wealth and when. Wealth, the success of businesses, jobs and careers are all incredibly uncertain. (1 Timothy 6:17) Most of the top 100 businesses that existed 100 years ago do not exist today. Certain careers that flourished 100 years ago do not exist today, and many houses and fortunes have been lost due to disaster, war, bad health, misfortune, etc. For many of us, becoming wealthy is something that at best will lead us to become unfruitful (Mark 4:19), and at worst will lead us away from God altogether. So, in most cases, God will not give you the wealth that you desire or think that you need.

> *When you have eaten and are satisfied, praise the Lord your God for the good land He has given you. Be careful that you do not forget the Lord your God, failing to observe His commands, His laws and His decrees that I am giving you this day. Otherwise, when you eat and are satisfied, when you build fine houses and settle down, and when your herds and flocks grow large and your silver and gold increase and all you have is multiplied, then your heart will become proud and you will forget the Lord your God, who brought you out of Egypt, out of the land of slavery. He led you through the vast and dreadful desert, that thirsty and waterless land, with its venomous snakes and scorpions. He brought you water out of hard rock. He gave you manna to eat in the desert, something your fathers had never known, to humble and to test you so that in the end it might go well with you. You may say to yourself, "My power and the strength of my hands have produced this wealth for me." But remember the Lord your God, for it is He who gives you the ability to produce wealth, and so confirms His covenant, which He swore to your forefathers, as it is today.* (Deuteronomy 8:10-18)

For some, God will allow all our wealth to be taken away for some greater reason as in the case of Job, who has inspired many by his faithfulness. For others like Moses, Joseph and David, they were stripped of their wealth to mold their character in preparation to becoming great leaders for God's great people.

C. Wealth Comes For A Reason

Wealth and honor come from you; you are the ruler of all things. In your hands are strength and power to exalt and give strength to all. Now, our God, we give you thanks, and praise your glorious name. "But who am I, and who are my people, that we should be able to give as generously as this? Everything comes from you, and we have given you only what comes from your hand. We are aliens and strangers in your sight, as were all our forefathers. Our days on earth are like a shadow, without hope. O Lord our God, as for all this abundance that we have provided for building you a Temple for your Holy Name, it comes from your hand, and all of it belongs to you. (1 Chronicles 29:12-16)

Wealth comes for a reason; to give it away. There is always a purpose for God's blessings, a need or a role prepared in advance for us to meet. (Ephesians 2:10) Our money and wealth belong not to us but to God, and as such, we must always be asking God what we should do with it and not what we want to do with it. When we have wealth and it is in our power to help God's cause, we are not to withhold from giving. (Proverbs 3:27) We are to be rich towards God. (James 5:1-3; Luke 12:21)

Point II: The Ups And Downs Of Wealth

While we all crave security, knowing we can pay our bills or the bills of the future, life so often is just not like that. Sometimes we lose money and it is our own fault; occasionally it is because of misfortune (Ecclesiastes 5:13-14); and in other cases, God allows us to lose our wealth to further His cause or teach us a lesson. Therefore, we must have increasing faith in the fact that God really loves us and will take care of us.

A. The Case Of Lot

Now Lot, who was moving about with Abram, also had flocks and herds and tents. But the land could not support them while they stayed together, for their possessions were so great that they were not able to stay together. (Genesis 13:5-6)

Lot was the nephew of Abraham and under his guidance Lot acquired wealth as did Abraham. In fact, Abraham and Lot were so blessed, that the land could not support them both. Lot became independent of Abraham and immediately made a bad decision by living next to Sodom.

Abram lived in the land of Canaan, while Lot lived among the cities of the plain and pitched his tents near Sodom. Now the people of Sodom were wicked and were sinning greatly against the Lord. (Genesis 13:12-13)

In time, we then find Lot not just living next to Sodom but living in Sodom.

The four kings seized all the goods of Sodom and Gomorrah and all their food; then they went away. They also carried off Abram's nephew Lot and his possessions, since he was living in Sodom. (Genesis 14:11-12)

Lot had gone from being guided by a spiritual man to being enticed by worldly people. He was living in a city and surrounding himself with sin. The consequence was that Lot was taken captive by sinful men losing all his possessions and wealth. Because of God's grace and Abraham's courage, Lot was rescued by his uncle with his possessions. (Genesis 14:16) God was teaching Lot a great lesson here: To not get close to ungodly people. So it is with us, God will use the loosing of our wealth to teach us a lesson. When this happens, as my brother Kip says, "We must become better Christians not bitter Christians!"

B. The Case Of Job

In the land of Uz there lived a man whose name was Job. This man was blameless and upright; he feared God and shunned evil. He had seven sons and three daughters, and he owned seven thousand sheep, three thousand camels, five hundred yoke of oxen and five hundred donkeys, and had a large number of servants. He was the greatest man among all the people of the East. (Job 1:1-3)

Job was the greatest man of the East, incredibly wealthy, blameless and upright. Then God allowed Satan to take away his wealth by allowing bandits to run off with his oxen, donkeys and camels. Then fire from Heaven burned up his sheep and servants and wind blew over his family property. (Job 1:8-20) Wealth can be lost in a moment if God so desires or allows it. Yet the inspiring thing about Job is how he reacted. It was unlike so many today who lose everything and turn to sin or suicide. Job turned to God. Job was willing to be used as an example for us all. Just like Christ, he suffered so we could learn from his example. The question we must ask ourselves is, "Are we happy to be used in such a way, to go through hardship and respond in such a godly manner that inspires others to be godly?" Once the hardship had served its purpose, God then blessed Job's life twice as much as before.

After Job had prayed for his friends, the Lord made him prosperous again and gave him twice as much as he had before. (Job 42:10)

C. The Case Of David

David began his life as the youngest of eight sons. He was probably given all the hand me downs and the most difficult jobs. (1 Samuel 16:11) He then became the hero of all Israel by killing Goliath. He was given a high rank in Saul's army. Then because of Saul's jealousy, David had to flee for his life, leaving his possessions and even his wife. On one occasion, David had to survive among his enemies by pretending to be mad. At one point, while he led a band of dubious men, his home was burned down, his possessions stolen, and his family captured. God graciously allowed David to get all his possessions and family safely back again. (1 Samuel 30) David was later made king, and then lost it all as his son Absalom rebelled against him. In time, David regained his wealth and died with wealth.

> *He died at a good old age, having enjoyed long life, wealth and honor. His son Solomon succeeded him as king.* (1 Chronicles 29:28)

Yet in all this David learned many valuable lessons that he has passed on to us.

> *I was young and now I am old, yet I have never seen the righteous forsaken or their children begging bread. They are always generous and lend freely; their children will be a blessing.* (Psalms 37:25-26)

> *The blameless spend their days under the Lord's care, and their inheritance will endure forever. In times of disaster they will not wither; in days of famine they will enjoy plenty.* (Psalms 37:18-19)

Point III: The Principles Of Giving To God And God Replenishing What You Have Given

When looking at any topic in Scripture, including how to view and use your wealth, there must always be a healthy fear of God. Not only is God in control of your life, but He will also reward and punish a man for the way he conducts his life.

When living in Los Angeles, my friend David Caldwell gave a very short but profound talk at church about giving. He shared how he was asked by a young trainee minister if he had any money because the minister had over stretched himself financially on faith by meeting a man to study the Bible. The trainee minister only had enough money to get to the Bible study but not get home, so he asked Dave to help him. The only money David had was the money he needed to get to work the next day. Despite that, David willingly gave the young minister his money. The next day, David got up early because he had to now walk the long distance to work. As he walked he began to pray and then found a $50 USD bill on the ground, far more than he had given the young minister.

> *And without faith it is impossible to please God, because anyone who comes to Him must believe that He exists and that He rewards those who earnestly seek Him.*
> (Hebrews 11:6)

A. Principle Of Generosity

> *One man gives freely, yet gains even more; another withholds unduly, but comes to poverty. A generous man will prosper; he who refreshes others will himself be refreshed. People curse the man who hoards grain, but blessing crowns him who is willing to sell.* (Proverbs 11:24)

The world says to hold onto your money and you will prosper; God says exactly the opposite. Most people live to save up wealth for hard times and for their retirement. God says use your money to save others and I will make you prosper. The way that God views things and the way the world views things, even the way the religious world views things, are in stark contradiction and opposition of each other.

> *For the message of the cross is foolishness to those who are perishing, but to us who are being saved it is the power of God. For it is written: "I will destroy the wisdom of the wise; the intelligence of the intelligent I will frustrate." Where is the wise man? Where is the scholar? Where is the philosopher of this age? Has not God made foolish the wisdom of the world? For since in the wisdom of God the world through its wisdom did not know Him, God was pleased through the foolishness of what was preached to save those who believe.* (1 Corinthians 1:18-21)

B. The Principles Of God Withholding From Those Who Withhold From Him, And Giving To Those Who Give To Him

> *Honor the Lord with your wealth, with the firstfruits of all your crops; then your barns will be filled to overflowing, and your vats will brim over with new wine.*
> (Proverbs 3:9-10)

God gives after we give to Him, not before. God does not want the leftovers but wants you to put Him first.

> *"I the Lord do not change. So you, O descendants of Jacob, are not destroyed. Ever since the time of your forefathers you have turned away from my decrees and have not kept*

them. Return to me, and I will return to you," says the Lord Almighty. "But you ask, 'How are we to return?' "Will a man rob God? Yet you rob me."

"But you ask, 'How do we rob you?'"

"In tithes and offerings. You are under a curse – the whole nation of you – because you are robbing me. Bring the whole tithe into the storehouse, that there may be food in my house. Test me in this," says the Lord Almighty, "and see if I will not throw open the floodgates of Heaven and pour out so much blessing that you will not have room enough for it. I will prevent pests from devouring your crops, and the vines in your fields will not cast their fruit," says the Lord Almighty. "Then all the nations will call you blessed, for yours will be a delightful land," says the Lord Almighty. (Malachi 3:6-12)

God withheld blessings from Israel as a nation because they withheld from Him and from the poor, widows and foreigners. (Deuteronomy 14:28-29) God asks them to test Him to see if He will bless them. For a person to believe the Scriptures about being blessed by God, he must first obey them. Only then will he see that God's Word is indeed true.

> *Give, and it will be given to you. A good measure, pressed down, shaken together and running over, will be poured into your lap. For with the measure you use, it will be measured to you.* (Luke 6:38)

Jesus teaches the same principle under the New Covenant regarding giving first to God and then as a result, He will bless you. How you treat God and others is how He will treat you. God will use those around you in your job, neighborhood, university and family to discipline you, as all people are God's chosen instruments.

C. Not Giving Into Fear That God Will Not Come Through For You

There is no fear in love. But perfect love drives out fear, because fear has to do with punishment. The one who fears is not made perfect in love. We love because He first loved us. (1 John 4:18-19)

Fear is the main reason men do not give to God or refuse to let go of their wealth. Common thoughts are, "What if I get into trouble financially?" or "What if it goes wrong or I get into debt?" Yet we must ask ourselves, "Does God love me? Will He come through for me?" The answer should be yes, but we will only know if we put ourselves in a situation where we need Him to come through for us.

Yet it was good of you to share in my troubles. Moreover, as you Philippians know, in the early days of your acquaintance with the Gospel, when I set out from Macedonia, not one church shared with me in the matter of giving and receiving, except you only; for even when I was in Thessalonica, you sent me aid again and again when I was in need. Not that I am looking for a gift, but I am looking for what may be credited to your account. I have received full payment and even more; I am amply supplied, now that I have received from Epaphroditus the gifts you sent. They are a fragrant offering, an acceptable sacrifice, pleasing to God. And my God will meet all your needs according to His glorious riches in Christ Jesus. (Philippians 4:14-19)

The Macedonian Churches gave to the Apostle Paul, and he thanked them and reminded them that God will meet their needs, despite and because of their sacrifice. When we are fearful to give, we must not focus on how little we have left, but on how big is our Benefactor.

Conclusion

It's all about faith; faith in the power of God, faith in the love of God, faith that God's Word and His way are true and always work.

> *I have been crucified with Christ and I no longer live, but Christ lives in me. The life I live in the body, I live by faith in the Son of God, who loved me and gave Himself for me.* (Galatians 2:20)

You must believe that:

1. God gives you wealth.
2. You will be able to handle the ups and downs of wealth with God.
3. When you hold onto the principle of giving to God, God will replenish what you have given Him.

Chapter 8
Faith And Money

Introduction

When I first became a Christian in 1990, I was eager to give from the heart out of gratitude for God's love and His church and from a logical point of view. I lived in London and earned £700 a month, and as a non-Christian, I spent a large proportion of this on getting drunk, smoking and other ungodly activities. So now that these sins were no longer in my life, I had money freed up, which made giving £70 a month a logical step of gratitude for me. However, over the coming months, I moved out of a relative's apartment where I had been living and started having to pay rent and bills. The cost of life in London hit home quickly. The brothers' household that I moved into was a long distance from work. Travel costs grew, and while I was having the time of my life, I started having to really watch my finances and make choices on what I could and could not do because I was just getting by every month. During one service I heard a short talk on contribution that changed my life. It went something like this:

> *Clearly no one is justified before God by the Law, because, "The righteous will live by faith." The Law is not based on faith; on the contrary, "The man who does these things will live by them."* (Galatians 3:11-12)

After reading this profound Scripture, the speaker went on to ask, "Are you giving to God according to what you can afford? How powerful do you think your God is? I want to challenge you to give more than you can afford and watch God work!"

Short and simple but impacting! So that night, I raised my weekly contribution by £5 a week. I then calculated how much that would be per year – £260. I walked into work the next day and asked to see my boss. I explained to him that my living expenses had gone up and I needed a pay raise. He asked me how much, and I told him £260 a year and he gave me a pay raise of that amount!

> *In the same way, faith by itself, if it is not accompanied by action, is dead.* (James 2:17)

Over that 24 hours, I learned so many lessons. God is loving and powerful. I was worth more to my boss than I thought, which encouraged me. I could have been giving more to God for some time up to that point if I simply had more faith. This one event changed the way I looked at God, money, my career and life overall. Since then I have never doubted God's willingness to provide for me when I am putting Him and His Kingdom first. In fact, the only time God challenges man to test Him is in this area of giving. (Malachi 3:10)

Point I: Seeing Your Life From God's Point Of View Not Yours

> *While Jesus was in one of the towns, a man came along who was covered with leprosy. When he saw Jesus, he fell with his face to the ground and begged Him, "Lord, if you are willing, you can make me clean."*
> *Jesus reached out His hand and touched the man. "I am willing," He said. "Be clean!" And immediately the leprosy left him.* (Luke 5:12-13)

So often we are like this man, asking God "if" He is willing to help us. The real question is not, "Is God willing?" but "Are you willing to trust God?"

A. God Has So Much Wealth At His Disposal

After Jesus and His disciples arrived in Capernaum, the collectors of the two drachma tax came to Peter and asked, "Doesn't your teacher pay the Temple tax?" "Yes, he does," he replied.

When Peter came into the house, Jesus was the first to speak. "What do you think, Simon?" He asked. "From whom do the kings of the earth collect duty and taxes from their own sons or from others?"

"From others," Peter answered.

"Then the sons are exempt," Jesus said to him. "But so that we may not offend them, go to the lake and throw out your line. Take the first fish you catch; open its mouth and you will find a four drachma coin. Take it and give it to them for my tax and yours." (Matthew 17:24-27)

This is one of my favorite stories where I see the humor of God. Jesus and His disciples are challenged to give a tax based on Exodus 30:13 and Jesus uses this as a time to teach Peter. Rather than pay the tax out of what money they have, He instructs Peter to go with the talents He has (fishing), put them to work, and expect God to do a miracle. The first fish that he catches will have the money in its mouth.

I imagine Peter setting off and, on his way, being asked by the disciples, his wife or other fishermen what he is doing. Peter then must explain that Jesus told him to fish and that he will pull money from the first fish's mouth. How would they have responded? How would Peter have felt telling them this? Would they have come to watch?

This scene played out would make for a great comedy skit. I imagine Peter slowly pulling the fish to shore, grabbing the fish, opening the fish's mouth, maybe while closing his eyes, only to see the coin appear. Then he gets up before the crowd and proudly shows the coin to all the onlookers saying, "Told you so!" Peter would return to Jesus, wondering if he should confess his lack of faith before he caught the fish. I imagine Peter giving the coin over to the tax collectors in front of Jesus, only to see Jesus wink or smile.

God knows where every fallen coin is, where every hidden treasure is buried, and where all the wealth in the world could be found and given to you. The issue is not can God provide financially for you, but why does He not provide for you. Growing up, I lived in a small village in the county of Suffolk in England. Throughout my youth I often walked, cycled and drove through another village just a few miles away called Hoxne. In that village laid a buried treasure known now as the Hoxne Hoard. It contained over 14,000 gold, silver and bronze Roman coins. It was found in 1992 and is worth over three million English pounds today. I passed that treasure countless times, and God could have directed me to it through me falling off my bike or in some more spiritual way like going for a prayer in the field. The only problem was, that at that time in my life I did not have a relationship with Him, so I would not have been willing to be directed by Him. So, He directed someone else to find it.

When entering the Promised Land, the tribe of Zebulun's blessing from Moses was to be a tribe that feasted on treasure hidden in sands.

> *About Zebulun [Moses] said: "Rejoice, Zebulun, in your going out, and you, Issachar, in your tents. They will summon peoples to the mountain and there offer the sacrifices of the righteous; they will feast on the abundance of the seas, on the treasures hidden in the sand."* (Deuteronomy 33:18-19)

B. If You Do Not Ask You Do Not Get

Ask and it will be given to you; seek and you will find; knock and the door will be opened to you. For everyone who asks receives; he who seeks finds; and to him who knocks, the door will be opened.

Which of you, if his son asks for bread, will give him a stone? Or if he asks for a fish, will give him a snake? If you, then, though you are evil, know how to give good gifts to your children, how much more will your Father in Heaven give good gifts to those who ask Him! (Matthew 7:7-11)

So often we do not ask God because we think that He is too busy, unloving or does not care about us. Nothing could be further from the truth. My father has always given me birthday gifts, Christmas gifts and gifts when he went away. I was constantly on his mind, just like with our Heavenly Father. We are constantly on His mind and He wants to love us.

I have learned to constantly ask for things for free and expect God to provide. Even when at McDonald's, I love embarrassing my kids by asking the cashier if the food is free today. When renting a venue, I ask if we can rent their venue for free for church because it is for God as we are a charity. For 18 months, the Sydney Church was blessed to meet in an all-purpose church that seated 400 in the city center for only $100 a week. I did ask to have it for free and while the whole church prayed, God determined $100 would be the final cost. Interestingly, the hotel on the opposite side of the road would have been $2,000. This extremely low rent enabled us to hire more staff to preach the Gospel and grow His Kingdom more quickly.

God is on our side. We must live like He is. I have received free beds, washing machines, furniture, a car, televisions and even canoes. I know that these were given to me through God's hand, not to hoard, but to give away to the needy or sell online to provide financially.

C. Give Up Everything To Gain Everything

A certain ruler asked Him, "Good teacher, what must I do to inherit eternal life?" "Why do you call me good?" Jesus answered. "No one is good – except God alone. You know the commandments: 'Do not commit adultery, do not murder, do not steal, do not give false testimony, honor your father and mother.'"
"All these I have kept since I was a boy," he said.
When Jesus heard this, He said to him, "You still lack one thing. Sell everything you have and give to the poor, and you will have treasure in Heaven. Then come, follow me."
When he heard this, he became very sad, because he was a man of great wealth. Jesus looked at him and said, "How hard it is for the rich to enter the Kingdom of God! Indeed, it is easier for a camel to go through the eye of a needle than for a rich man to enter the Kingdom of God."
Those who heard this asked, "Who then can be saved?"
Jesus replied, "What is impossible with men is possible with God." (Luke 18:18-27)

If ever there was a story that showed that God expects us to give up everything and in return He will not only provide for today but always, it is the rich young ruler. (Mark 10:17-31; Matthew 19:16-30) The rich young ruler is taken totally off guard by Jesus's call to wholehearted commitment to God. Jesus called him to give away the very thing that he put his hope and trust in – his money and wealth, every penny – and rely totally on God! Even the disciples were taken aback and quickly professed that is what they had done.

Peter said to Him, "We have left all we had to follow you!"
"I tell you the truth," Jesus said to them, "no one who has
left home or wife or brothers or parents or children for the
sake of the Kingdom of God will fail to receive many times
as much in this age and, in the age to come, eternal life."
(Luke 18:28-30)

Jesus then helps them to focus not on what they had given up, but on what they would receive. Some would have to give up wives, children and homes, yet Jesus promises that they will not only receive eternal life but will also receive back much more here on earth. We too often find ourselves like a child with their father who refuses to let go of a broken toy he is asking for, in order that he can replace it with a brand-new toy. I often wonder how that rich young ruler felt years later, maybe he still went on to lose all the wealth that he so highly valued, possibly through misfortune or mismanagement. Did he end up regretting that moment when God tested him, and he failed? We only know that he will deeply regret his lack of faith on judgement day.

We must always ask ourselves why we hold on so tightly to what we have when God can so richly bless us with so much more. Like a full glass of water, it will only hold so much unless it is emptied. It cannot have any more poured into it. So, it is with our lives. Unless we constantly empty ourselves of the possessions and the wealth we have, there is simply no room for God to work.

Point II: God Will Meet Your Needs

A. Learning To Depend On God Not Yourself

During the forty years that I led you through the desert,
your clothes did not wear out, nor did the sandals on your
feet. You ate no bread and drank no wine or other

fermented drink. I did this so that you might know that I am the Lord your God. (Deuteronomy 29:5-6)

When the Israelites came out of Egypt, God was trying desperately to build a relationship with them as a nation. Indeed, He was trying to teach them not only what was right and wrong through the Law, but He also wanted them to trust Him. Trust is a deep root of love and without trust there is no real love. (1 Corinthians 13:7) The most practical way for God to do this was to take everything away from them and provide for them daily. Just like children today, even when they quarrel with their parents, they cannot deny that their parents love them, because they provide food, clothes and shelter for them. In the Western world, we are so infatuated with independence that if we cannot work out how to provide for ourselves then we believe that no one can. Yet in many people's lives who are farmers, fishermen or hunters, they easily see their need for external help from God because they know so much of their success comes from events outside their control. These people and cultures often have more of a "God focus" than those based in the cities where jobs seem more "man dependent."

When Jesus taught His disciples to pray in Luke 11, He taught them to pray to God to meet their daily needs, *"Give us this day our daily bread."* For this prayer to be applicable, you need to know what your daily needs are, pray for them, and expect God to deliver them. When you cannot see how you can meet your needs, that does not mean they will not be met. No need to grumble, it is just time to pray.

B. God Wants To Take Care Of His Children

And God is able to make all grace abound to you, so that in all things at all times, having all that you need, you will abound in every good work. As it is written: "He has scattered abroad His gifts to the poor; His righteousness endures forever."

Now He who supplies seed to the sower and bread for food will also supply and increase your store of seed and will enlarge the harvest of your righteousness. You will be made rich in every way so that you can be generous on every occasion, and through us your generosity will result in thanksgiving to God. (2 Corinthians 9:8-11)

This verse so beautifully describes how God will provide for us: *"He is able," "in all things at all times," "having all that you need," "[giving] His gifts to the poor," "He who supplies," "increase your store," "enlarge the harvest," "you will be made rich in every way,"* and *"you can be generous on every occasion."* It is all about God loving and caring for us. When we believe God loves us deeply, we will look for how He can and has provided for us. When we think He is not loving, our self-pity or disbelief often leads us to a lack of action. Where others see God working, some only see doom and certain failure.

I remember being at a wedding and seeing that the church was clearing out their church hall. They were throwing out two canoes in a large rubbish bin, so I spoke to a friend who promptly helped me take the canoes home after the wedding. We then sold them and had some extra money with which we could be generous to others. There are always gifts scattered around by God, you just have to look for them and believe they are from God.

C. God Loves To Rescue His Children

No one can serve two masters. Either he will hate the one and love the other, or he will be devoted to the one and despise the other. You cannot serve both God and Money. Therefore I tell you, do not worry about your life, what you will eat or drink; or about your body, what you will wear. Is not life more important than food, and the body more important than clothes? Look at the birds of the air; they do not sow or reap or store away in barns, and yet your Heavenly Father feeds them. Are you not much more valuable than they? Who of you by worrying can add a single hour to his life?

And why do you worry about clothes? See how the lilies of the field grow. They do not labor or spin. Yet I tell you that not even Solomon in all his splendor was dressed like one of these. If that is how God clothes the grass of the field, which is here today and tomorrow is thrown into the fire, will He not much more clothe you, O you of little faith? So do not worry, saying, "What shall we eat?" or "What shall we drink?" or "What shall we wear" For the pagans run after all these things, and your Heavenly Father knows that you need them. But seek first His Kingdom and His righteousness, and all these things will be given to you as well. Therefore do not worry about tomorrow, for tomorrow will worry about itself. Each day has enough trouble of its own. (Matthew 6:24-34)

Most people do not believe that they love money or that it is their master. Yet your master is the person or thing that you think about most. So, ask yourself what consumes your heart and mind the most? If you are always worried about how you will pay the bills, give your contribution, get the next possession, then this is what is mastering you. Yet, if you are truly at peace in knowing that God will provide, then you will not be worried in heart or speech. Ask some of your friends, "Do I worry about money? Do I talk about my fears of making ends meet or how God or the church asks for too much?" If so, God is not your master, money is. I learned a long time ago, that God is a rescuer.

He rescues and He saves; He performs signs and wonders in the Heavens and on the earth. He has rescued Daniel from the power of the lions. (Daniel 6:27)

The only challenge with God being a rescuer is that He wants to put you in a position of needing to be rescued. With nearly all the great stories of the Bible, someone needed rescuing before the miracle came, as in the cases of Moses parting the Red Sea and David killing Goliath. This is the same with your financial needs. You need to be in a place of trouble to be rescued by God. If you seek His righteousness and His Kingdom, He promises to meet your every daily need.

I have been rescued financially in so many ways by God, big and little, from getting extra money from friends, family, strangers, work and even finding money as I walked along the street. I have sold things for more than I bought them. I have seen possessions on the side of the road and sold them. I have found possessions such as furniture and household goods to provide for Christians in need. There are even free advertisements now for items being given away. The ways that God provides are endless if we would only believe, pray and act on God-given opportunities.

If you, then, though you are evil, know how to give good gifts to your children, how much more will your Father in Heaven give good gifts to those who ask Him! (Matthew 7:11)

Point III: Giving It All Up Again And Again And Again

A. The Cost Of Following Godly Leadership

After King Solomon died, the Kingdom of God split into two: The tribes of Judah and Benjamin under Rehoboam who were based in

Jerusalem, and all the other tribes of Israel under Jeroboam centered at the city of Shechem. Jeroboam then turned away from God, so the priest and Levites left their ungodly leader to go to be in Judah. This cost them all their land and property.

> *The priests and Levites from all their districts throughout Israel sided with Rehoboam. The Levites even abandoned their pasturelands and property, and came to Judah and Jerusalem because Jeroboam and his sons had rejected them as priests of the Lord. And he appointed his own priests for the high places and for the goat and calf idols he had made.* (2 Chronicles 11:13-15)

When I was a young Christian, I happily gave up everything (Luke 14:33) and moved for the sake of the Gospel. I could fit most of my possessions in a suitcase or car. However later in life, I bought a house, furniture, special ornaments for the house and even acquired some equity in my house. I was in a church that I thought was doing what was right, yet over time it became clear that it was lukewarm and had abandoned some of the Biblical principles that I believed and zealously practiced as a young Christian. This is something that God takes very seriously. (Revelations 3:15-17)

The problem was, after considering other local churches, and seeing their lukewarmness, the one I believed God was calling me to was in another country! The only way to get there was to self-finance our family through a religious working visa. I was 44 years old and this meant spending what money we had saved and giving up shares my employer had recently given me conditional on my next three years of employment. Financially, it was a bad decision, a cost of $140,000, but spiritually, an essential decision that would change the course of our lives. The struggle for me was that somehow, I had convinced myself that giving up everything for God was either a onetime thing at conversion or something young people did, not a reoccurring pattern for my whole life. My wife and I had to read this verse nearly every day just to get through it.

> *"I tell you the truth," Jesus said to them, "no one who has left home or wife or brothers or parents or children for the sake of the Kingdom of God will fail to receive many times as much in this age and, in the age to come, eternal life."* (Luke 18:29-30)

We did move all the way from Sydney to Los Angeles. Now we have seen many souls won for Christ because of our decision, not least of which are those in the Sydney Church that God used us to plant. Lord wiling, in turn, the Sydney Church will plant churches throughout Australia and the countries around Australia including China, the largest nation in the world at 1.4 billion lost souls.

B. Letting Go Of Bad Decisions

> *Amaziah called the people of Judah together and assigned them according to their families to commanders of thousands and commanders of hundreds for all Judah and Benjamin. He then mustered those twenty years old or more and found that there were three hundred thousand men ready for military service, able to handle the spear and shield. He also hired a hundred thousand fighting men from Israel for a hundred talents of silver.*
> *But a man of God came to him and said, "O king, these troops from Israel must not march with you, for the Lord is not with Israel, not with any of the people of Ephraim. Even if you go and fight courageously in battle, God will overthrow you before the enemy, for God has the power to help or to overthrow."*

Amaziah asked the man of God, "But what about the hundred talents I paid for these Israelite troops?"
The man of God replied, "The Lord can give you much more than that."
So Amaziah dismissed the troops who had come to him from Ephraim and sent them home. They were furious with Judah and left for home in a great rage.
(2 Chronicles 25:5-10)

Here we find the King of Judah, Amaziah – who was striving to do what was right in the sight of God – make a bad decision. He hired men of Israel, as he thought God was with and asked them to fight with him. He paid a lot of money to do this. God, through a man of God, told Amaziah that it was a bad decision. Amaziah's first thought was about the money that he would lose. (The exact amount in today's money is disputable but consider how much it would cost to hire 100,000 men today for a week to clean up a construction site. That would be a lot of money in any country. Very likely, the cost to hire the Israelite soldiers would have been much more than that.) God's advice through his prophet was to focus not on the amount he was losing, but on God, who could supply him with wealth. The prophet said, *"The Lord can give you much more than that."* Losing money due to following God takes faith, courage and often upsets people, but it is still the right decision. If the king had disobeyed for fear of the men being furious with him or for greed to not lose his investment, he may well have sent the Israelite soldiers to their deaths.

C. Contentment In All Situations

I rejoice greatly in the Lord that at last you have renewed your concern for me. Indeed, you have been concerned, but you had no opportunity to show it. I am not saying this because I am in need, for I have learned to be content whatever the circumstances. I know what it is to be in need, and I know what it is to have plenty. I have learned the secret of being content in any and every situation, whether well fed or hungry, whether living in plenty or in want. I can do everything through Him who gives me strength. (Philippians 4:10-13)

Paul's life was one of financial ups and downs, yet he mastered the ability to not let that bother him. Often, we get into a mentality that once we have reached a certain standard in life, we try to hold on to it at the cost of our spiritual life. Lowering our standard of living can do wonders for our heart.

When I was a student, if I found a television on the side of the road, I would take it home. Then I would see if it worked, and if it had a blue line through the screen, I did not throw it out; I praised God that I had a television that worked. Yet after I gained wealth, things that were a little broken or not quite right, started to bother me. I am so glad that God has called me to go back to the mission field, because I noticed how unspiritual that I had become about possessions. When I had new things such as couches and other pieces of furniture, it bothered me when people spilt something on them or mistreated them, and I would be angry in my heart, that in turn would damage my relationships with people. Now I am back somewhat to furniture that is either old or I have received it free, so when friends or their children come over and stain, crack or dent my possessions, I have a different attitude. They just go along with the other stains, cracks and dents. The desire for nice things so often makes you an "un-nice" person.

Conclusion

We...

1. Must see our lives from God's point of view, not ours.
2. Know that God will meet our needs.
3. Must have the faith to give it all up again and again and again.

Jesus taught His disciples again and again that they were to depend on Him even when they had little or even nothing.

> *Then Jesus asked them, "When I sent you without purse, bag or sandals, did you lack anything?" "Nothing," they answered."* (Luke 22:35)

Nothing + God = Needs Met

Chapter 9
Motivating Yourself And Others To Give To God

Introduction

Before you can start motivating anyone to give to God, you must first deal with your own heart and life. Men and women follow courage, faith and personal example.

> *When the princes in Israel take the lead, when the people willingly offer themselves, praise the Lord!* (Judges 5:2)

This is the ideal state of any group of godly people; the leaders take the lead, and the people following them willingly.

Point I: You Cannot Fake It To Make It

A. Be Honest With Yourself

> *For a man's ways are in full view of the Lord, and He examines all his paths.* (Proverbs 5:21)

For most people reading this, the issue is not can you give or give more, but do you not want to? We eat out, have vacations, choose to buy brand name clothes and we live a life of excess not survival. Be honest! Are you the most frugal, cost-minded, sacrificial person you know? Do you always say "no" to what you want and only buy what you need? Is your wardrobe only full of two pairs of shoes, two outfits, etc. We are brought up in a society that says that it is good to have what you want and not just what you need. For most, the issue is not can we give or give more in regular contributions or to one-off special needs and contributions? The issue is more likely, why do I not want to give more? Why do a lot of people not like to be talked to about giving more? Is it because they do not want to feel challenged to give more? Or is it that they may have a more discomforting lifestyle? Is it that it will require more discipline? Feelings will pop up like "I have already given enough" and "Why do I have to be so sacrificial when others are not?"

If you can pinpoint the real reason you do not want to give or give more, then you have a starting point from which to grow. When you grow in giving more, then you have a point from which you can teach others. Before we can teach, we must have learned. If you give more by becoming more disciplined, then you can teach others to be more disciplined. If you give more by letting go of some of your life's wants, then you can teach others to do the same. If you give more by increasing your faith, then you can teach others to increase their faith.

B. Get Open With God And Someone Else

Dealing with our heart is the most difficult thing we can do as a Christian. Unless we learn to do this well, we will be constantly deceived by our own heart and as a result, not do what God wants us to do. This could also lead us to live a life that does not measure up to the vision God has for us. When you find the root of why you have any resistance in your heart, then you can go to God about it just like Jesus at Gethsemane. (Mark 14:32-42) You take your heart to God and ask Him to change your will into His will. You can also get open with others, not trying to justify why you should not give more but getting open with the person or people you know that have a strength in this area that will call you higher. Do not look to share with people who do not help you grow spiritually for fear of being challenged. What I find normally happens is one of two things. When speaking to spiritually-minded people, they either help you by sharing a Scripture that helps you make the decision you know you need to make, or they give you a different perspective that you have not thought about that helps you decide.

> *As iron sharpens iron, so one person sharpens another.* (Proverbs 27:17)

> *And Saul's son Jonathan went to David at Horesh and helped him find strength in God.* (1 Samuel 23:16)

C. Decide To Live By Faith Not By Sight

The righteous live by faith, not by sight. God does not want us to base our decisions on human reasonings which leads to rationalizations. These thoughts are often based on our past experiences. He wants us to excel in all things and that also means excelling in giving, to go beyond where we are at presently, to transcend our present thinking, to outgrow our present selves, to improve upon and to even shock ourselves by our growth.

> *But just as you excel in everything in faith, in speech, in knowledge, in complete earnestness and in your love for us see that you also excel in this grace of giving.* (2 Corinthians 8:7)

As you excel in your prayer life with God, as you grow in your knowledge of Him, as you draw closer to God, this in turn should help you excel more and more in giving to Him and His Kingdom. Decide today to grow more. When you do, and God blesses you and teaches you something, you can then share it with others. This will start the process of you learning to motivate those around you. The key to inspiration is acknowledging that you too struggle and then sharing how you overcame it. As you share, people gain hope and faith that they too can change. The more you share your story, the more your faith will grow inside of you and others. You will inspire yourself to grow again, and again, and again, which will reflect in those you lead.

Point II: You Cannot Help Others Change Unless You Have Changed

A. Example Is Everything

> *Was it a sin for me to lower myself in order to elevate you by preaching the Gospel of God to you free of charge? I robbed other churches by receiving support from them so as to serve you. And when I was with you and needed something, I was not a burden to anyone, for the brothers who came from Macedonia supplied what I needed. I have kept myself from being a burden to you in any way, and will continue to do so.* (Corinthians 11:7-9)

Paul led by example. He was hard working; he was a good steward of his money and possessions, so that he did not burden those he led through a lack of discipline or bad decisions. People follow examples more than words or commands. It has often been said that people have already chosen whether to listen to a speaker by reviewing their life and seeing if their life matches up to their words. If it does not, they do not take your words seriously. This is why Jesus had such an impact as opposed to the Pharisees. Jesus said come follow me and watch what I do, then imitate. The Pharisees told people what to do, but their lives did not match their teaching, and they were not willing to help people by showing them how to overcome their challenges.

> *The teachers of the Law and the Pharisees sit in Moses' seat. So you must be careful to do everything they tell you. But do not do what they do, for they do not practice what they preach. They tie up heavy, cumbersome loads and*

put them on other people's shoulders, but they themselves are not willing to lift a finger to move them. (Matthew 23:2-4)

The first rule of leading is to lead by example. If you call others to give, then give first. If you are starting a project to raise money, start it before anyone else so people can see how it can be done. Do things that inspire yourself and others. Scare yourself by doing something that only God can help you achieve. Simply put, leaders are meant to lead from the front not push from behind. No one likes being pushed. It is an example that inspires people to action.

B. Give Lots And Lots And Lots Of Practicals

Generally speaking, Christians have great hearts and want to give. They want their friends and families to be saved through their giving. They want to do great things for God and for less fortunate people, but most people are not that creative. I find the most creative people are simply those who have been exposed to lots of creative ideas and remembered them. I would not say I am very creative, but I once heard someone say, "Originality is forgetting where you got if from." I have struggled at times as much as the next guy to give money, to raise money and to give more money. Yet, one thing that I decided to do early on in my spiritual life, was to master how to raise money by seeking out the solutions that other people had used successfully and imitate them. There is no excuse for us today to not find solutions; just Google: "Top 100 ways to raise money" or "100 ways to raise money for charity" or "100 ways for teens to make money." The Internet will give you an abundance of solutions and ideas on how to raise money effectively.

One example of a creative idea was when Keira of the Sydney Church visited a professional cupcake maker. She learned how to make amazing cupcakes and then taught us how to make these luxurious cupcakes with incredible icing. The following Saturday, my family and I simply set up a stall to sell cupcakes at the end of our street, and we raised hundreds of dollars in a day. We also came to know our neighbors.

The other key issue is providing examples that work in "your" situation. What works in one country may not work in another. What works in one city, one culture, one group of people, or one family does not necessarily work in another. Provide an overwhelming list of opportunities for people from which to choose. Find a solution to fit your situation. This is the exact opposite of Matthew 23:4.

C. Discipling Not Preaching

Leading well takes a lot of hard work and getting your hands dirty with individuals. I have seen many leaders and ministers fail to help the groups they lead to grow, to change and to meet a need because they simply preach the solution from the pulpit in the hope that their groups "gets it." Instead, you must get into people's lives on a one-to-one basis to *"teach, rebuke, correct and train people in righteousness."* (2 Timothy 3:16) Preaching from pulpit rarely gets the job done. Just like Jesus, we are to take a few and train them to train others. One-on-one discipleship is how we teach people to obey rather than just teaching people the facts. (Matthew 28:20)

The most common statement that I have heard when financial issues are addressed only from the pulpit instead of one-on-one is, "They do not understand my situation." What people want is to be listened to, understood and then given a "tailor made solution" just for them.

You cannot do this speaking to a crowd, only by one-on-one. The larger the group you lead, the harder it is, but it is still the most effective way.

One instance where I saw this work practically was a when a burdened sister came up to me after hearing about a need to give in the church. All the members were encouraged to raise a certain amount for the mission field. I knew her to have a great heart and felt sad that she felt burdened about this. Kerry and I spent time with her and she said that she wanted to give but thought she could only raise half the amount. I encouraged her that I knew she would do all that was possible. I told her I knew she loved God and He loved her, and that sometimes we as a family need to cover each other's hard times. As her leader, I promised that I would work hard to raise the amount she could not. Well come the collection day, she gave far more than what she had originally thought she could! As well, it did my heart good to give beyond what I thought I could, as I had raised extra money for this sister.

To move people's hearts, you must personally touch people many, many times because when people feel loved and believed in they will astound you in what they will do. For most young people, it takes giving them a specific plan and then holding them accountable by regular encouragement. For those who know how to already do it, it is normally just about making sure they are doing well spiritually.

Point III: Language Is Everything

A. Enthusiasm Is Key

> *For I know your eagerness to help, and I have been boasting about it to the Macedonians, telling them that since last year you in Achaia were ready to give; and your*

enthusiasm has stirred most of them to action.
(2 Corinthians 9:2)

If there is any reservation in you about personally giving, talking about giving or calling people to give, most will sense it, see it and know it. It will greatly lessen your effectiveness in motiving people. If you do not know how raise funds yourself, you cannot give practicals. If you as the leader are reluctant to give for any reason, your group will not own their responsibility of getting or giving the money. Faithless statements will abound such as, "My leader says we need to raise…" or "In an ideal world we will be able to raise…"

One of the most challenging amounts I have ever had to give and help people raise per person was $72,000 AUS from 30 people in the second year of the Sydney Church. The need was clear. The number was exact. Yet, I felt it a tremendous honor to be called by God to be used to do something I knew was going to take faith, love, hard work and result in bringing great glory to God. I also looked at the people that I was leading and knew that when we completed the task, they would have grown spiritually beyond what they thought possible. I took a night to explain to the church how the need had come about, and to teach them how God expected us to respond to such "opportunities." I shared how excited I was to be tested by God in this way in regard to my leadership. Then I gave the practicals on how my wife and I were going to do our part. The church enthusiastically set about attacking the issue. God provided, our faith grew, and God was glorified!

Kerry and I decided to give out of the savings that we had saved up for our children's education as I felt God was testing me to trust Him to replenish it. We gave $10,000 AUS! A lot for us! Yet only two months later God – through the government – gave us $12,000 AUS in back payments for children's allowance that I did not know that we could claim. For others, they worked hard in taking up extra shifts, and as I shared before, one sister became the "cupcake queen" and raised an astounding amount.

To this day, it is the standard that we look back on in the Sydney Church, and like Moses parting the Red Sea to get Israel out of trouble, it is part of the history of how the movement in Sydney started. Now when we talk about raising funds in Sydney, there is an excitement and "wow" about what God will do, as opposed to a "sigh" about what we have been asked to do.

I have been questioned on multiple occasions why I get so excited about facing financial challenges. There are some challenges that we get into due to our own sin. These I never get excited about, but the ones that are thrust upon us by unseen circumstances or needs that pop up, I always see as being given by God. Therefore, if they are given by God, He must want me to:

1. Walk in faith as He provides the solution, and as I watch Him do it I stand in awe of His power, which always excites me.

2. Redirect my finances. This may mean that Kerry and I will be giving more and spending less, which makes me more like Jesus.

3. Search hard in the Scriptures for a similar situation in the Bible where He has given this challenge before and I have missed it. Once I find it, I can imitate how the righteous dealt with it. Then I understand the heart of God more.

4. Redirect my life. When the finances in Sydney were seemingly in trouble, I was surrendered to going back out to full-time work like the Apostle Paul when he went back to tent making. I thought maybe there was someone who needed converting that God wanted to use me to get to through a job, or maybe He wanted someone else to lead His church.

What I do know is that God is in control and leads His church, not me. I must simply focus on loving Him and willingly let Him direct all aspects of my life.

> *And we know that in all things God works for the good of those who love Him, who have been called according to His purpose.* (Romans 8:28)

B. Knowledge Is Motivating

When there is a financial challenge, explain clearly how much money is needed or expected. Explain clearly what the money will be used for and why so that trust is built. Then there is no room for anyone to be suspicious of where the money is going. Attach the money to the actual cause, to people and places. In the example of Sydney, it was easy for me to show the church our budget, where the money would go, and who had been converted because of the last money raised. When raising money inside a large church, it often helps Christians to allocate their funds to a certain mission field so that mission field can then send letters, photos and emails of how previous money was spent and where future money will be spent, on whom, why and the impact it is prayerfully going to have.

C. Pleasant Words Motivate

> *The wise in heart are called discerning, and pleasant words promote instruction.* (Proverbs 16:21)

If you only use words or expressions such as "must," "have to," "obey," "duty" or "God commands," while all those are true, they will normally only motivate those who are not struggling to give. The ones that need motivating are those who for whatever reason lack faith, are struggling to be disciplined with their own finances, and/or have a wounded heart in some way. These are the people who need you to inspire them to do what is right. Be careful when using words like "must" or "duty" as they are the sort of words wounded hearts can view as harsh and harsh words only stir up anger not obedience. (Proverbs 15:1) These are Bible words but combine them with other words that are inspiring.

Let us learn from a master motivator regarding how to encourage and inspire others to give, as the Apostle Paul speaks to the Christians in the Corinthian Church:

> *And now, brothers, we want you to know about the grace that God has given the Macedonian Churches. Out of the most severe trial, their overflowing joy and their extreme poverty welled up in rich generosity. For I testify that they gave as much as they were able, and even beyond their ability. Entirely on their own, they urgently pleaded with us for the privilege of sharing in this service to the saints. And they did not do as we expected, but they gave themselves first to the Lord and then to us in keeping with God's will. So we urged Titus, since he had earlier made a beginning, to bring also to completion this act of grace on your part. But just as you excel in everything – in faith, in speech, in knowledge, in complete earnestness and in your love for us – see that you also excel in this grace of giving.*

> *I am not commanding you, but I want to test the sincerity of your love by comparing it with the earnestness of others. For you know the grace of our Lord Jesus Christ, that though He was rich, yet for your sakes He became poor, so that you through His poverty might become rich.*

And here is my advice about what is best for you in this matter: Last year you were the first not only to give but also to have the desire to do so. Now finish the work, so that your eager willingness to do it may be matched by your completion of it, according to your means. For if the willingness is there, the gift is acceptable according to what one has, not according to what he does not have. Our desire is not that others might be relieved while you are hard pressed, but that there might be equality. At the present time your plenty will supply what they need, so that in turn their plenty will supply what you need. Then there will be equality, as it is written: "He who gathered much did not have too much, and he who gathered little did not have too little."

I thank God, who put into the heart of Titus the same concern I have for you. For Titus not only welcomed our appeal, but he is coming to you with much enthusiasm and on his own initiative. And we are sending along with him the brother who is praised by all the churches for his service to the Gospel. What is more, he was chosen by the churches to accompany us as we carry the offering, which we administer in order to honor the Lord Himself and to show our eagerness to help. We want to avoid any criticism of the way we administer this liberal gift. For we are taking pains to do what is right, not only in the eyes of the Lord but also in the eyes of men.

In addition, we are sending with them our brother who has often proved to us in many ways that he is zealous, and now even more so because of his great confidence in you. As for Titus, he is my partner and fellow worker among you; as for our brothers, they are representatives of the churches and an honor to Christ. Therefore show these men the proof of your love and the reason for our pride in you, so that the churches can see it. There is no need for me to write to you about this service to the saints. For I know your eagerness to help, and I have been boasting about it to the Macedonians, telling them that since last year you in Achaia were ready to give; and your enthusiasm has stirred most of them to action.

But I am sending the brothers in order that our boasting about you in this matter should not prove hollow, but that you may be ready, as I said you would be. For if any Macedonians come with me and find you unprepared, we, not to say anything about you, would be ashamed of having been so confident. So I thought it necessary to urge the brothers to visit you in advance and finish the arrangements for the generous gift you had promised. Then it will be ready as a generous gift, not as one grudgingly given.

Remember this: Whoever sows sparingly will also reap sparingly, and whoever sows generously will also reap generously. Each man should give what he has decided in his heart to give, not reluctantly or under compulsion, for God loves a cheerful giver. And God is able to make all grace abound to you, so that in all things at all times, having all that you need, you will abound in every good work. As it is written: "He has scattered abroad His gifts to the poor; His righteousness endures forever." Now He *who supplies seed to the sower and bread for food will also supply and increase your store of seed and will enlarge the harvest of your righteousness. You will be made rich in every way so that you can be generous on every occasion, and through us your generosity will result in thanksgiving to God.*

This service that you perform is not only supplying the needs of God's people but is also overflowing in many expressions of thanks to God. Because of the service by which you have proved yourselves, men will praise God for the obedience that accompanies your confession of the Gospel of Christ, and for your generosity in sharing with them and with everyone else. And in their prayers for you their hearts will go out to you, because of the surpassing grace God has given you. Thanks be to God for His indescribable gift! (2 Corinthians 8:1-9:15)

Paul's language here is full of compliments not rebukes, encouragements not threats, inspiring truths not harsh realities. All you have to do is to read this passage out loud to yourself to hear them. These verses are full of expressions that motivate; *"Overflowing joy," "extreme poverty," "rich generosity," "urgently pleaded," "he is zealous," "though He was rich, yet for your sakes He became poor," "I know your eagerness to help," "your enthusiasm has stirred most," "Whoever sows generously will also reap generously," "for God loves a cheerful giver," "You will be made rich in every way," "Because of the service by which you have proved yourselves, men will praise God."*

After hearing a speech like this, who would not be inspired to give?

D. Constantly Thank People

Christians give again and again and again. One of the things that we often forget to do is thank them again and again and again. Yes, giving wholeheartedly is what God expects, but nonetheless it is always nice to hear a thank you or an appreciation. We are often quick to point out when someone does not give, but the key to motivating people to keep giving is to make them feel appreciated. After all, Christians are volunteers not employees. Paul takes considerable time in his letter to the Philippian Church to thank them for their gifts long after they had been received. As well, Paul also made their generosity known to all, holding them up as an example. How encouraging would that have been?

> *Yet it was good of you to share in my troubles. Moreover, as you Philippians know, in the early days of your acquaintance with the Gospel, when I set out from Macedonia, not one church shared with me in the matter of giving and receiving, except you only; for even when I was in Thessalonica, you sent me aid again and again when I was in need. Not that I am looking for a gift, but I am looking for what may be credited to your account. I have received full payment and even more; I am amply supplied, now that I have received from Epaphroditus the gifts you sent. They are a fragrant offering, an acceptable sacrifice, pleasing to God. And my God will meet all your needs according to His glorious riches in Christ Jesus.*
> (Philippians 4:14-19)

E. A Time To Command

> *Command those who are rich in this present world not to*

be arrogant nor to put their hope in wealth, which is so uncertain, but to put their hope in God, who richly provides us with everything for our enjoyment. Command them to do good, to be rich in good deeds, and to be generous and willing to share. In this way they will lay up treasure for themselves as a firm foundation for the coming age, so that they may take hold of the life that is truly life. (1 Timothy 6:17-19)

There is a time to command people to give; when people are rich, and they are not giving generously. You must take time to sit down with the rich and explain that they are rich and that they are not being generous. If they are not giving generously, ironically, they most probably think that what they are giving is generous. This may take talking specifically about income, possessions, investments and holidays. Do not be afraid to talk about these things as greed is a deadly sin. (Ephesians 5:3-6) It is sad how out of touch we can become of the plight of the poor. We become so wrapped up in what we want and can do with "our" money that we lose touch with the reality.

Leaders must be like Nehemiah, as he unapologetically addressed the rich of his day – *"the nobles and officials"* – who were disconnected from the plight of the poor. (Nehemiah 5:1-19) It takes bold leadership to deal with and to motivate the rich to be generous.

Conclusion

Then the Lord raised up judges, who saved them out of the hands of these raiders. (Judges 2:16)

If people did not need motivating to do what is right, then we would not need leaders. However, we all need leadership, inspiration and encouragement. As leaders, we need to become expert motivators of ourselves and others since hearts are fragile.

Remember when motivating:

1. You can't fake it to make it.
2. You can't help others to change unless you have changed.
3. Language and tone are everything and will carry the day.

SECTION FOUR

MINI STUDIES

Chapter 10
Dealing With Money And Contribution At Conversion

The following 12 chapters are studies that incorporate all the principles in the first nine chapters of this book.

How we deal with people at conversion makes a huge difference in their early years as a Christian, and it often affects them even beyond that time. How and what we teach them about giving contribution, missions fund raising, and special contributions is crucial. Some people are afraid to talk about money which can lead to a lack of conviction on the issue in new converts. We are not to recommended giving just "something" or refer to giving 10% of our income with the expectation that this is enough. We must also be careful when talking about being sacrificial and the New Covenant standard of giving everything that we do not miss the heart of the matter, which is generosity.

We must take each person case by case. If a person earns $200,000 a year and only gives $20,000 a year – which would be 10% – that may be a lot of money to the person studying the Bible with them, but it is not a lot of the person's wealth and may not be generous toward God. If the person is a single mother of five kids giving $50 a week when she earns $500 a week, this may be incredibly generous toward God, but it also may be beyond her ability to sustain this level of giving.

God gives us many great examples of how Jesus dealt with people's hearts regarding wealth and possessions at their calling; Peter the fisherman gave up his career (Luke 5:1-11), Levi the tax collector left everything (Luke 5:27-29), Zacchaeus the chief tax collector radically repented in his view of money and possessions (Luke 19:1-10), and the rich young ruler who was lovingly confronted by Jesus but unwilling to give up everything. (Luke 18:18-26) Too many Christians grumble about giving their wealth, for some it is because it was not dealt with thoroughly at conversion. If it was dealt with thoroughly, they most likely would not be struggling with this issue now. We must never be afraid to deal with the issue of money at conversion, even if it means that person turns away from the truth. Jesus never shied away from it.

Below is a short and useful study to help people deal with money at conversion.

Study: Giving Your Wealth To God

Today we are going to talk about giving money to God and using your wealth to further His Kingdom.

> *In the same way, those of you who do not give up everything you have cannot be my disciple.* (Luke 14:33)

Q: What is Jesus saying here?
Q: What does He mean by giving up everything?
Q: Does everything mean possessions and wealth?
Q: How do you feel about that?
Q: How do you feel about giving money to God to further His work in this congregation and on the mission field?

Let us look at one of Jesus' early conversions in the Bible.

> *Jesus entered Jericho and was passing through. A man was there by the name of Zacchaeus; he was a chief tax collector and was wealthy. He wanted to see who Jesus was, but being a short man he could not, because of the crowd. So he ran ahead and climbed a sycamore fig tree*

to see Him, since Jesus was coming that way. When Jesus reached the spot, He looked up and said to him, "Zacchaeus, come down immediately. I must stay at your house today." So he came down at once and welcomed Him gladly. All the people saw this and began to mutter, "He has gone to be the guest of a 'sinner. '"

But Zacchaeus stood up and said to the Lord, "Look, Lord! Here and now I give half of my possessions to the poor, and if I have cheated anybody out of anything, I will pay back four times the amount."

Jesus said to him, "Today salvation has come to this house, because this man, too, is a son of Abraham. For the Son of Man came to seek and to save what was lost." (Luke 19:1-10)

Q: How did Zacchaeus respond to being called by Jesus?

Q: Why do you think he responded this way?

Q: If Zacchaeus was able to give half his possessions to the poor, how many possessions do you think he had that he did not need?

Q: Who have you lived for in your life up to now?

Q: How many possessions do you have that you do not really need?

Q: How much of your wealth has been spent just on you with no eternal goal?

Q: What did Jesus state His mission was and therefore what yours should be?

Challenge: Once you become saved, you cannot become more saved only more effective at converting people and this includes using your wealth to save others. (Luke 16:9)

For Christ's love compels us, because we are convinced that one died for all, and therefore all died. And He died for all, that those who live should no longer live for themselves but for Him who died for them and was raised again. (2 Corinthians 5:14-15)

Q: According to this verse who should we live for?
Q: What should compel us to do all things as a Christian?
Q: Does that include giving financially?

Then Jesus said to them, "Watch out! Be on your guard against all kinds of greed; a man's life does not consist in the abundance of his possessions."

And He told them this parable: "The ground of a certain rich man produced a good crop. He thought to himself, 'What shall I do? I have no place to store my crops.' Then he said, 'This is what I'll do. I will tear down my barns and build bigger ones, and there I will store all my grain and my goods.' And I'll say to myself, 'You have plenty of good things laid up for many years. Take life easy; eat, drink and be merry.'"

But God said to him, "You fool! This very night your life will be demanded from you. Then who will get what you have prepared for yourself?" This is how it will be with anyone who stores up things for himself but is not rich toward God. (Luke 12:15-21)

Q: What is greed? (Greed is the desire for excess possessions, wealth and food.)
Q: How much has greed been a part of your life up to now?
Q: How much money do you think you would save a week or month if you dealt with your greed?
Q: What do you think it means to be rich toward God?

A generous man will prosper; he who refreshes others will himself be refreshed. (Proverbs 11:25)

Q: What does God promise in Proverbs 11:25?
Q: What does it mean to prosper?
Q: In which areas of your life would you like to prosper?
Q: Do you believe that being generous is the key to prosperity?

Remember this: Whoever sows sparingly will also reap sparingly, and whoever sows generously will also reap generously. Each man should give what he has decided in his heart to give, not reluctantly or under compulsion, for God loves a cheerful giver. And God is able to make all grace abound to you, so that in all things at all times, having all that you need, you will abound in every good work. As it is written: "He has scattered abroad His gifts to the poor; His righteousness endures forever."

Now He who supplies seed to the sower and bread for food will also supply and increase your store of seed and will enlarge the harvest of your righteousness. You will be made rich in every way so that you can be generous on every occasion, and through us your generosity will result in thanksgiving to God. (2 Corinthians 9:6-11)

Q: What does it mean to sow generously versus sowing sparingly?
Q: According to God what is the key to reaping generously?
Q: According to this passage, if you give generously will all of your needs be met?
Q: If a Christian is poor, what do these Scriptures teach that God Will do for them? (God will give them gifts, enlarge their harvests, and be made rich in every way.)
Q: Why does God make Christians rich in every way? (So, they can be

generous.)

Q: Does God want you to give reluctantly or sparingly?

In the church, we have three areas of giving:

1. Benevolence

> *For Macedonia and Achaia were pleased to make a contribution for the poor among the Lord's people in Jerusalem. They were pleased to do it, and indeed they owe it to them. For if the Gentiles have shared in the Jews' spiritual blessings, they owe it to the Jews to share with them their material blessings.* (Romans 15:26-27)

We give benevolence at Midweek Service to meet the needs of the Christians going through difficult times. This is just like what the early church did. How do you feel about giving to help those in need in your church family?

2. Missions

As you know, we are called to fulfill the great commission in Matthew 28:18-20. We are dedicated to evangelizing the world in our generation. In the first and second worlds, this means sending out mission teams and supporting them until they are self-supporting. For third world congregations, there is almost always the need for ongoing support. To meet these needs, we raise money every year to support these efforts. How do you feel about raising money or giving extra to save the whole world? (Share practically how you have personally done this and how much fun it has been.) How do you feel about helping to raise money to send out mission teams and funding established third world churches?

3. Weekly Contribution

In our family of churches – the SoldOut Movement – we take up a weekly contribution for the running of the local church. This pays for the rental of meeting places, the staff and ministry expenses such as hosting visiting speakers, food for events, and buying invitations. These expenses are shown in a yearly financial presentation to the whole church. How do you feel about setting aside a generous amount of your income to support the work of God's church?

Conclusion

I want you to take these Scriptures and look at what you earn and consider what would be a generous amount for you to give for weekly contribution toward the running of the church? What would it mean for you to be rich toward God and what you would like to give to help those in need? Take this decision before God in prayer. Then decide between God and you how much you will pledge to Him and His Kingdom on a weekly basis. How do you feel about doing this?

When we get together next, please let me know the decision that you have made between you and God.

I am going to leave you with these verses to encourage you:

> *No one can serve two masters. Either you will hate the one and love the other, or you will be devoted to the one and despise the other. You cannot serve both God and Money. Therefore I tell you, do not worry about your life, what you will eat or drink; or about your body, what you will wear. Is not life more than food, and the body more than clothes? Look at the birds of the air; they do not sow or reap or store away in barns, and yet your Heavenly Father feeds them. Are you not much more valuable than they?*

Can any one of you by worrying add a single hour to your life?

And why do you worry about clothes? See how the flowers of the field grow. They do not labor or spin. Yet I tell you that not even Solomon in all his splendor was dressed like one of these. If that is how God clothes the grass of the field, which is here today and tomorrow is thrown into the fire, will He not much more clothe you – you of little faith? So do not worry, saying, 'What shall we eat?' or 'What shall we drink?' or 'What shall we wear?' For the pagans run after all these things, and your Heavenly Father knows that you need them. But seek first His Kingdom and His righteousness, and all these things will be given to you as well. Therefore do not worry about tomorrow, for tomorrow will worry about itself. Each day has enough trouble of its own. (Matthew 6:24-34)

Chapter 11
Fulfilling Your Contribution Pledge To God

Each man should give what he has decided in his heart to give, not reluctantly or under compulsion, for God loves a cheerful giver. (2 Corinthians 9:7)

When we become a Christian, we must understand that what we give financially is to God and not to man or the church. It is essential that we take the decision of what we give to God very seriously, praying it through, and then deciding with God what we will promise to give Him. This is a continual process as our finances increase, and as a result should be reflected in an increase in our pledge to God. There are times when this may on occasion need to be adjusted in a decrease. Again, this is something we would need to speak to God about as well as to seek godly advice.

Yet after we have made a pledge to God, we need to understand that God takes your word to Him seriously. We take God at His Word and He takes us at ours. We hold on to His Word and His promises, and subsequently, He holds us to ours.

If you make a vow to the Lord your God, do not be slow to pay it, for the Lord your God will certainly demand it of you and you will be guilty of sin. But if you refrain from making a vow, you will not be guilty. Whatever your lips utter you must be sure to do, because you made your vow freely to the Lord your God with your own mouth.
(Deuteronomy 23:21-23)

When you make a vow to God, do not delay in fulfilling it. He has no pleasure in fools; fulfill your vow. It is better not to vow than to make a vow and not fulfill it. Do not let your mouth lead you into sin. And do not protest to the [Temple] messenger, "My vow was a mistake." Why should God be angry at what you say and destroy the work of your hands?" (Ecclesiastes 5:4-6)

Lord, who may dwell in your Sanctuary? Who may live on your holy hill? He whose walk is blameless and who does what is righteous, who speaks the truth from his heart and has no slander on his tongue, who does his neighbor no wrong and casts no slur on his fellowman, who despises a vile man but honors those who fear the Lord, who keeps his oath even when it hurts. (Psalms 15:1-4)

"Cursed is the cheat who has an acceptable male in his flock and vows to give it, but then sacrifices a blemished animal to the Lord. For I am a great king," says the Lord Almighty, "and my name is to be feared among the nations." (Malachi 1:14)

The issue is integrity. God did not make you pledge a certain amount, it was what you decided. When trouble, hardship or even God's discipline comes your way, this is not a reason to give way to fear, faithlessness or double-mindedness and not bring the firstfruit of your wealth to God. After all, we honor worldly commitments such as our rent to our landlord, bank payments for a car, electric company bills, etc. God is watching to see what you will do under pressure.

I know, my God, that you test the heart and are pleased with integrity. All these things have I given willingly and with honest intent. And now I have seen with joy how willingly your people who are here have given to you.
(1 Chronicles 29:17)

Jesus reminded us of the simplicity of it all.

> *Again, you have heard that it was said to the people long ago, "Do not break your oath, but keep the oaths you have made to the Lord." But I tell you, Do not swear at all: either by Heaven, for it is God's throne; or by the earth, for it is His footstool; or by Jerusalem, for it is the city of the Great King. And do not swear by your head, for you cannot make even one hair white or black. Simply let your "Yes" be "Yes," and your "No," "No;" anything beyond this comes from the evil one.* (Matthew 5:33-37)

When we decide to give a certain amount to God, it cannot be, "I will give dependent on my job, my wealth, my income or the economy." The Scriptures teach us that if you say you will give a certain amount to God, then simply give it.

> *Above all, my brothers, do not swear, not by Heaven or by earth or by anything else. Let you "Yes" be yes, and your "No," no, or you will be condemned.* (James 5:12)

Conclude the study with the following illustration. You may want to use your own example instead.

The Case Of Pete

On the Sydney Mission Team in 2014, my friend Pete came into a position where he held on to the Scriptures and God blessed his integrity. In coming to Australia from America, life was financially tough for him and many others. Getting a job was difficult despite Pete being a very qualified architect. That said, Pete had personally saved up money to come on the mission team. The first few months while he was looking for a job, he gave a generous amount in weekly contribution to help fund the newly planted Sydney Church. Pete used his savings to rent a house as well, but as these funds ran low and the only work he could secure was sporadic – washing pots in a restaurant – he came to a point where his income could not pay his rent and his contribution. This was emotionally trying for Pete as he was in his late twenties and had integrity. What should he do?

Pete prayed and wanted to honor his decision to God to give what he had pledged. This meant not being able to pay his rent. He communicated regularly with his landlord, explaining his situation and that he was looking for better work. This situation went on for a few weeks. The church did give Pete some initial benevolence but could not give it as an ongoing payment. Pete never stopped giving to God what he had decided, even when that meant losing his apartment. He moved in with brothers who helped support him for a short time. Pete constantly communicated with the landlord until he paid back his arrears in rent.

In those first seven months of the mission team, Pete who is an intelligent, respectable and qualified professional, was humbled by God and stripped of his money and his ability to provide for himself. Yet, he never lost his integrity to God. It was only then that God blessed him with finding a job for $147,000 AUS, a sum that Pete could never have dreamed of in his own country of America! He was able to pay off his debt and then increased his contribution to God. A few criticized Pete for being irresponsible, not fulfilling his duties to his landlord before his God. Some told him that he should lower his contribution or not give it for a few weeks. Pete has always believed that his giving to God is about his relationship with God. It involves trust, hope, loyalty and faith. Pete is a God-focused man, and I for one count it a privilege to have him as a friend. I am pretty sure God feels the same way!

Supplementary Practicals For Leaders

As a Shepherd of the church, I realize that people's giving reflects their relationship with God. Therefore, I constantly look at the finances of the church and who gives what, like Jesus watching His people place their contributions into the Temple boxes. As different individuals gave their contribution, Jesus spoke to His disciples to teach them.

> *Jesus sat down opposite the place where the offerings were put and watched the crowd putting their money into the Temple treasury. Many rich people threw in large amounts. But a poor widow came and put in two very small copper coins, worth only a few cents. Calling His disciples to Him, Jesus said, "Truly I tell you, this poor widow has put more into the treasury than all the others. They gave out of their wealth; but she, out of her poverty, put in everything – all she had to live on."* (Mark 12:41-44)

What am I looking for when I review the giving each week? Well, I am primarily looking for who is in trouble and not being open about it. Some people get very embarrassed when they overspend or hit hard times and do not want to let anyone know. If we do not know they are in trouble, then how can we love and help them? When I see that someone does not give contribution that week, I ask them if everything is ok? If not, I ask, how can I or we as a church help them? We must love one another deeply to care for each other. (1 John 3:17)

The next thing that I am concerned about is how they are doing spiritually. Over the years as a leader, I have noticed a pattern that those who leave the Lord often stop giving financially weeks beforehand. Not giving is often an outward sign of an inward problem. So again, I call the disciple to set up time with them to get them spiritually strong. (Of note here: If the only time that you get with people is when they do not give their contribution, they can feel your love is insincere. So, it is a good reminder to get with all your flock regularly.) The next thing I focus on is character. What you do once, you most likely will do again, then again and again and again, until it becomes your character. So, a repeated lack of integrity in not giving or having integrity and repeatedly giving, are both a matter of character.

> *When the sentence for a crime is not quickly carried out, people's hearts are filled with schemes to do wrong.* (Ecclesiastes 8:11)

When we allow ourselves to not deal with issues in our own life and of those we lead in the church, we do ourselves and them a great disservice. Our role is not to simply help people get saved, it is to get them to Heaven – *"[bearing] fruit that will last."* (John 15:16) There is a far-reaching principle that must be talked about when a disciple lacks integrity. If a Christian has no problem withholding their gift to God, and have not sought out a plan, advice or solution to deal with it, we must in love address this. Of concern, what other areas of their life will they lack integrity, and in the future, how will that affect them, their marriage and their family?

Jesus said after a person is baptized, *"...Teach them to obey everything I have commanded you."* (Matthew 28:20) We are to be like fathers and mother who are loving enough to deal with the root issues, not a hired hand that deals with only the outward sign of the root issue.

> *For you know that we dealt with each of you as a father deals with his own children, encouraging, comforting and*

urging you to live lives worthy of God, who calls you into His Kingdom and glory. (1 Thessalonians 2:11-12)

We must train people to be disciplined and to understand the impact of bad decisions in small ways so that these character flaws do not lead to larger problems in the future. Teach a person to have integrity in small things, like giving weekly contribution – *"even when it hurts"* – and you will train them how to do well in all areas of life.

Chapter 12
Increasing Your Giving

Introduction

And now, brothers, we want you to know about the grace that God has given the Macedonian Churches. Out of the most severe trial, their overflowing joy and their extreme poverty welled up in rich generosity. For I testify that they gave as much as they were able, and even beyond their ability. Entirely on their own, they urgently pleaded with us for the privilege of sharing in this service to the saints. And they did not do as we expected, but they gave themselves first to the Lord and then to us in keeping with God's will. So we urged Titus, since he had earlier made a beginning, to bring also to completion this act of grace on your part. But just as you excel in everything, in faith, in speech, in knowledge, in complete earnestness and in your love for us, see that you also excel in this grace of giving. (2 Corinthians 8:1-7)

There is an expectation in the Bible from God that we should grow spiritually in faith, in our ability to speak about our faith, in our knowledge of God, in our love, and in our giving. Practically this means constantly increasing our desire to give, and as God blesses our generosity, then we should be constantly increasing our actual giving.

Point I: Why Do People Not Increase Their Giving

There are several reasons, some of which are the following:

A. They Think That They Should Give Just A Tithe

This is an Old Covenant teaching, not a New Covenant teaching. Therefore, these individuals believe if they are tithing, then that is all God requires of them.

B. No One Calls Them To Increase In Their Giving

They are not called to increase their giving, which takes teaching from Scripture. As well, they are not challenged to obey what is being taught.

C. They Do Not Understand The Need

Often, church leaders just assume that people understand the need to give more as the ministry expands. This simply is not true. Knowledge is a great motivator and so this message must be repeated.

There is a pattern of being called to give more in the histories of God's movements recorded in the Bible. Under the Old Covenant, Moses called the Israelites to increase their giving beyond their required sacrifices under the Law to pay for the Tabernacle. Under the New Covenant, we see the young evangelist Timothy admonished by Paul to go to certain people and command them to give more.

> *Moses said to the whole Israelite community, "This is what the Lord has commanded: From what you have, take an offering for the Lord. Everyone who is willing is to bring to the Lord an offering of gold, silver and bronze..."* (Exodus 35:4-5)

Command those who are rich in this present world not to be arrogant nor to put their hope in wealth, which is so uncertain, but to put their hope in God, who richly provides us with everything for our enjoyment. Command them to do good, to be rich in good deeds, and to be generous and willing to share. In this way they will lay up treasure for themselves as a firm foundation for the coming age, so that they may take hold of the life that is truly life. (1 Timothy 6:17-19)

Point II: Why People Are Willing To Increase Their Contribution

A. They See And Understand The Need And Want To Help

Do not withhold good from those to whom it is due, when it is in your power to act. (Proverbs 3:27)

When goodhearted disciples are explained the need and called to help, then they respond because they have a relationship with God and want to please Him.

All the believers were one in heart and mind. No one claimed that any of his possessions was his own, but they shared everything they had. With great power the Apostles continued to testify to the resurrection of the Lord Jesus, and much grace was upon them all. There were no needy persons among them. For from time to time those who owned lands or houses sold them, brought the money from the sales and put it at the Apostles' feet, and it was distributed to anyone as he had need.

Joseph, a Levite from Cyprus, whom the Apostles called

Barnabas (which means Son of Encouragement), sold a field he owned and brought the money and put it at the Apostles' feet. (Acts 4:32-37)

B. They Understand The Spiritual Law At Work With Their Giving: It Is Impossible To Out Give God

A generous person will prosper; whoever refreshes others will be refreshed. (Proverbs 11:25)

One person gives freely, yet gains even more; another withholds unduly, but comes to poverty. (Proverbs 11:24)

Remember this: Whoever sows sparingly will also reap sparingly, and whoever sows generously will also reap generously. Each man should give what he has decided in his heart to give, not reluctantly or under compulsion, for God loves a cheerful giver. (2 Corinthians 9:6-7)

And without faith it is impossible to please God, because anyone who comes to Him must believe that He exists and that He rewards those who earnestly seek Him. (Hebrews 11:6)

I tell you the truth," Jesus said to them, "no one who has left home or wife or brothers or parents or children for the sake of the Kingdom of God will fail to receive many times as much in this age and, in the age to come, eternal life. (Luke 18:29-30)

C. They Understand Who Is Really In Charge Of Their Wealth

The Lord sends poverty and wealth; He humbles and He exalts. (1 Samuel 2:7)

But remember the Lord your God, for it is He who gives you the ability to produce wealth, and so confirms His covenant, which He swore to your forefathers, as it is today. (Deuteronomy 8:18)

Jabez was more honorable than his brothers. His mother had named him Jabez, saying, "I gave birth to him in pain." Jabez cried out to the God of Israel, "Oh, that you would bless me and enlarge my territory! Let your hand be with me, and keep me from harm so that I will be free from pain." And God granted his request.
(1 Chronicles 4:9-10)

D. Their Income Has Increased Or Expenses Have Decreased, So They Have More

When our income increases, either by change of job or a pay raise, we should "want" to give more so God can do more. Another interesting opportunity is differing exchange rates if paid from abroad, we should be conscience of this and want to give more. Our living expenses decrease when fuel prices are lower, our rent changes, or we become more disciplined with our finances. Again, we should automatically want to give more because we can.

For you know the grace of our Lord Jesus Christ, that though He was rich, yet for your sakes He became poor, so that you through His poverty might become rich.

And here is my advice about what is best for you in this matter: Last year you were the first not only to give but

also to have the desire to do so. Now finish the work, so that your eager willingness to do it may be matched by your completion of it, according to your means. For if the willingness is there, the gift is acceptable according to what one has, not according to what he does not have.
(2 Corinthians 8:9-12)

Point III. Practicals On Calling People (Including Yourself) To Increase Their Giving

So, when and how do you call people to increase their giving? Well as with all things in Christianity, it should be something you do as part of your life, like praying, evangelizing and bringing people to church. However, we all need reminding to do these things from time to time.

> *And let us consider how we may spur one another on toward love and good deeds.* (Hebrews 10:24)

Here are some practicals that I have either implemented in the churches I have led or those I have seen implemented that work in different situations, though of course this list is not exhaustive.

A. Have A Yearly Time To Call People To Increase Their Contribution

Prepare disciple's hearts for the yearly call to increase their contribution by teaching a focused class series on such topics as "Money in The Bible," "How God Guides Us to Managing Our Finances," or "How to Get A Better Job and Do Better in Your Job." I find a three-week series to be optimum, and then call people to raise their contribution. Most people enjoy being taught how to better manage or increase their money before being asked to give.

169

B. The Individual Touch Is So Needed To Move Hearts

Get with everyone individually in your church or group and listen to them in regard to where they are at financially. Then get with them a second time to go through a tailor-made study you have prepared for them to help them in this area. While this is time consuming, it is often the most effective. Focus on one group at a time such as a house church group or Bible discussion group. Then share with the next group the impact of doing this with the previous group. This builds each group's faith as you progress.

C. Take An Evening To "Brain-storm" How To Raise Contribution

Have a night where you get a group together and brain-storm how everyone can raise their contribution. This is best done in small groups but produces great ownership of the issue particularly when this meeting is with the group's leadership.

D. Identify The Faithful "Increasers" And Let Them Teach And Share

Have the most effective givers and the most faithful givers deliver a combined lesson on how and why they have raised their contribution and can give so much.

E. Study A Book Together... Maybe This One

Have the church or your group study a book on God and finances for a month. Then have an evening where everyone shares what they learned before a call to raise the contribution.

F. Organized Focused Workshops

Consider, from time to time, having a weekly job workshop for those without jobs. Another suggestion is an ongoing group for everyone striving to get a better job. Some of the topics could be, "How To Ask For A Promotion At Work," "How To Look For A Better Job," "How To Increase Your Skills To Improve Your Chances Of Getting A Pay Rise," "How To Get Your Boss' Job If They Leave," and "Finding Out Which Companies Pay Better For The Job You Are Doing In Your Company."

Whatever tool or method we use, we must always make sure we focus on the heart of why we are doing it and not make the method a "law." What we are ideally doing is creating a culture within the church of consistent and growing gratitude toward God and His love for us expressed in our giving to Him and His Kingdom.

Conclusion

Today because there is always a need for an increase in contribution to meet the church's expanding needs – but also because we can – the question is, "By what amount can you increase your contribution?"

Let's not talk about what you cannot do, but what you can do.

Chapter 13
Our Responsibility To The Poor

There is no doubt from the Bible that we have a responsibility to help the poor of this world.

A. The Poor Inside Of God's Kingdom

However, there should be no poor among you, for in the land the Lord your God is giving you to possess as your inheritance, He will richly bless you, if only you fully obey the Lord your God and are careful to follow all these commands I am giving you today. For the Lord your God will bless you as He has promised, and you will lend to many nations but will borrow from none. You will rule over many nations but none will rule over you.

If there is a poor man among your brothers in any of the towns of the land that the Lord your God is giving you, do not be hardhearted or tightfisted toward your poor brother. Rather be openhanded and freely lend him whatever he needs... Give generously to him and do so without a grudging heart; then because of this the Lord your God will bless you in all your work and in everything you put your hand to. There will always be poor people in the land. Therefore I command you to be openhanded toward your brothers and toward the poor and needy in your land. (Deuteronomy 15:4-11)

It was never God's intention for any of His chosen people, the Israelites, to be poor. He would consistently give Israel enough for all their needs to be met. Yet sometimes poverty comes on people for different reasons, some from unforeseen circumstances (but God sees them coming), others from making bad decisions, laziness or accidents. The Israelites were called to freely give to all the poor among them. This same teaching was carried over into the church between Christians – the spiritual Israelites.

> *What good is it, my brothers, if a man claims to have faith but has no deeds? Can such faith save him? Suppose a brother or sister is without clothes and daily food. If one of you says to him, "Go, I wish you well; keep warm and well fed," but does nothing about his physical needs, what good is it? In the same way, faith by itself, if it is not accompanied by action, is dead. But someone will say, "You have faith; I have deeds." Show me your faith without deeds, and I will show you my faith by what I do.* (James 2:14-18)

Giving to the poor of the church was a focus of the leadership in the early church.

> *James, Cephas and John, those esteemed as pillars, gave me and Barnabas the right hand of fellowship when they recognized the grace given to me. They agreed that we should go to the Gentiles, and they to the circumcised. All they asked was that we should continue to remember the poor, the very thing I had been eager to do all along.* (Galatians 2:9-10)

> *After an absence of several years, I came to Jerusalem to bring my people gifts for the poor and to present offerings.* (Acts 24:17)

B. The Poor Outside Of God's Kingdom

If any of your fellow Israelites become poor and are unable to support themselves among you, help them as you would a foreigner and stranger, so they can continue to live among you. (Leviticus 25:35)

Not only are we expected to help those inside of God's Kingdom, but also foreigners and strangers, those not of God's Kingdom. Helping is to be a proactive. When we see others in need, we are to act; we are to speak up and defend the poor and needy.

Speak up for those who cannot speak for themselves, for the rights of all who are destitute. Speak up and judge fairly; defend the rights of the poor and needy. (Proverbs 31:8-9)

C. How Does God View It When We Do Not Help the Poor?

If a man shuts his ears to the cry of the poor, he too will cry out and not be answered. (Proverbs 21:13)

He who gives to the poor will lack nothing, but he who closes his eyes to them receives many curses. (Proverbs 28:27)

Whoever oppresses the poor shows contempt for their Maker, but whoever is kind to the needy honors God. (Proverbs 14:31)

In Deuteronomy 14 and 26, God speaks specifically of the portion of the tithes under the Old Covenant going to the storehouse, not only to feed the Levites but also the poor. So, part of the tithes given by the Israelites was designated for the poor.

At the end of every three years, bring all the tithes of that year's produce and store it in your towns, so that the Levites (who have no allotment or inheritance of their own) and the foreigners, the fatherless and the widows who live in your towns may come and eat and be satisfied, and so that the Lord your God may bless you in all the work of your hands. (Deuteronomy 14:28-29)

In Malachi 3, God was telling the Israelites they were cursed because they robbed Him by not following His ordinances and not having food in His storehouse for the foreigners, the fatherless and widows, as well as the Levites. If the Israelites were not going to love the poor, then God would make them poor and then they would know what it was like to be in need. However, if they provided for the poor, then God would provide for them. (Deuteronomy 27:19)

"I the Lord do not change. So you, O descendants of Jacob, are not destroyed. Ever since the time of your forefathers you have turned away from my decrees and have not kept them. Return to me, and I will return to you," says the Lord Almighty. "But you ask, 'How are we to return?' "Will a man rob God? Yet you rob me."
"But you ask, 'How do we rob you?'"
"In tithes and offerings. You are under a curse – the whole nation of you – because you are robbing me. Bring the whole tithe into the storehouse, that there may be food in my house. Test me in this," says the Lord Almighty, "and see if I will not throw open the floodgates of Heaven and pour out so much blessing that you will not have room enough for it. I will prevent pests from devouring your crops, and the vines in your fields will not cast their fruit," says the Lord Almighty. "Then all the nations will call you

blessed, for yours will be a delightful land," says the Lord Almighty. (Malachi 3:6-12)

God had previously destroyed people for being unconcerned about the poor and needy. This was among Sodom's sins:

> *Now this was the sin of your sister Sodom: She and her daughters were arrogant, overfed and unconcerned; they did not help the poor and needy. They were haughty and did detestable things before me. Therefore I did away with them as you have seen.* (Ezekiel 16:49-50)

We must take warning from Jesus' Parable of the Sheep and the Goats in Matthew 25:31-46. Those who ignored the poor were thrown into the lake of fire and those who ministered to the poor were given eternal life. Jesus was making this a salvation issue! Of course, the spiritual application of this parable is to evangelise to the hungry, the thirsty etc.

D. How Does God View It When We Do Help The Poor?

> *He who is kind to the poor lends to the Lord, and He will reward him for what he has done.* (Proverbs 19:17)

Giving to the poor is giving to God and He takes note of it. When Cornelius gave gifts to the poor, they came up to God as memorial offerings. (Acts 10:1-4)

> *The generous will themselves be blessed, for they share their food with the poor.* (Proverbs 19:17)

What is the Bible teaching us? Those who give to the poor can expect blessings, not necessarily from those to whom they give, but from God

Himself. Even if the needy are your enemy, give to them when they are in need.

> *If your enemy is hungry, give him bread to eat; and if he is thirsty give him water to drink; for so you will heap coals of fire on his head, and the Lord will reward you.*
> (Proverbs 25:21-22)

Jesus taught that there will be rewards in Heaven for those who give to the poor and sell their possessions to do so.

> *Sell your possessions and give to the poor. Provide purses for yourselves that will not wear out, a treasure in Heaven that will never fail, where no thief comes near and no moth destroys.* (Luke 12:33)

> *Jesus looked at him and loved him. "One thing you lack,"* He said. *"Go, sell everything you have and give to the poor, and you will have treasure in Heaven. Then come, follow me."* (Mark 10:21)

E. The Practicals Of Helping The Poor

There are many ways we can help the poor. First, with our personal money. When your church takes up benevolent collections for the poor in the church, be they in your immediate church or on a foreign mission field, do not withhold but give generously. We are to support the full-time staff and look after the poor, not just one or the other.

We should also help the poor with our time. In the projects that I have been involved in over the years, most of which have been in the first world, the poor are sometimes provided for financially by many groups or the government. But what many desire is someone to just love them, listen to them, respect them, and visit them. (Matthew 25:36) Setting a monthly time where you visit someone in need or help at an organized event to serve the poor will not only help others but enrich your life too.

Many people have talents that can be used to enormous effect to help the poor and needy. If you are going to work for most of your life, it is worth considering if the job you do has an impact on the poor. I have always admired doctors who give up well-paying jobs to work in hospitals in the third world for little money in comparison. You may not be able to do that, but you can use your talents in other ways: Cooking for the elderly in your area; inviting them to dinner; mowing their lawn; or financially adopting a child in the third world. The list of ways to help the poor is endless. Focus not on what you cannot do, but what you can.

Conclusion

The challenges that I would like to leave you with are the following:

1. Decide an amount of money that you will regularly give to help the poor and do it consistently.
2. Get involved in the lives of the poor in some way on a consistent basis; make it part of your life.
3. Review the job you are doing, and where possible, do a job that has an impact on the poor.

Chapter 14
Budgeting And Managing Money

There are many ways to manage your money and if yours is working for you then continue doing that. However, if you need help in managing your wealth, the following are some tips on how to budget.

1. Have A Budget

The most import thing about money is knowing what money you do and do not have. Then allocating what you have to give generously to God and pay the bills, which in turn, shows you what money you can or cannot spend.

2. Keeping To Your Budget

There are always many things that tempt you to break your budget and over spend: Desire for possessions; buying gifts for friends; desire to do things; going out; and the list goes on and on. The big issue is learning to say "no" to yourself, your friends, your spouse and even your beloved children. If you cannot afford something, you must let people know and not feel embarrassed. You may even teach them something in doing so. Do not use credit cards or other forms of loaning money to buy things that you simply cannot afford. This will lead to wasting money on interest charges. Only use credit cards if you know you can pay them off completely every month without incurring interest charges.

3. Building Savings Into Your Budget

Too often I hear people say that they are in debt because they had an unexpected bill: Their car broke down; the electric bill was more than they thought it would be; or there was an emergency need in the family. Unexpected bills or costs will always come throughout your life, so you must get in the habit of saving money each week or month so that when (not if) they happen you will be able to pay those expenses without going into debt. No matter how low your income is, always save something regularly.

4. Allocate Your Living Expenses Realistically

In budgeting, some people work out every little cost at the lowest possible level. Life does not work like this. You may think your grocery bill will come to exactly $100 every week, but that is not always true. Your electric bill will not be the lowest you have ever had, or the same as this time last year. Things change! So, if you think your electric bill will normally be $100, budget a little more just in case. Get input from your family. Many times, with a family budget, you do not have a grasp on the items that your spouse buys.

5. Build Grace Into Your Budget

As much as I pride myself on my discipline, I always overspend, even if it is on little things. So, what I do to give myself grace, I allocate a sum for my electricity bill into every month, although it only comes every three months. So, two out of every three months there is a little extra for when something happens with a car, with my kids, etc.

6. Look For Ways To Save Money In Your Budget

Every month, once my money is allocated for food, bills, etc., I set about seeing how I can save money with discounts, special offers or cheaper petrol. This is a mentality that I have had to cultivate as it does not come naturally for me. When I was younger, I felt it was all too much trouble to bother to do this, yet I have had many great examples of people in my life that have convinced me by their frugality in one area leading them to be generous in another. I particularly appreciate friends who would find out how to get cheap movie tickets and therefore have enough money to buy me one with their savings. Also, friends who would find cheap deals at restaurants which meant they could pay for my meal. These examples encouraged me as well as convicted me all at the same time.

7. Look For Ways To Increase Your Income

When it comes to your budget, you can either spend less or earn more. There are hundreds of ways to increase your income if you apply yourself: buying things and selling them for more on the internet; buying quality goods at yard sales and then selling them at your own yard sale; baking goods and selling them at work or school events; renting out a room in your house or your garage; tutoring; hosting jewelry parties; etc. With creativity and imitation, there are innumerable ways to increase your income. Many of these are great ways to evangelize and meet people, but all of this takes forethought, consistent planning and focus.

8. If Married Always Do Your Budget Together And Allocate Expenses To Each Other Fairly

Two heads are better than one. As well, accountability helps you to not over spend. Most people like to be free to do what they want with their money. Sometimes it is because it takes effort to be disciplined with money and we are all tempted to be emotionally lazy. If you do your finances together, you not only have more advice to help you make better decisions, but you also instill some accountability to not over spend.

9. Never Go Into Debt (Romans 13:10)

If you are in debt, then restrict your living until you are out of debt. Debt incurs interest, sometimes at extreme costs. This is simply wasting your money. Get out of debt as quickly as possible and stay out of debt.

10. Track Your Spending

Know what you are spending as an individual and as a family. Have at least a weekly time to sit down and review your spending and projected spending. This catches problems early.

I have provided a basic sample weekly budget. It is simple because I believe that the simpler it is, the easier it is to follow.

Basic Sample Weekly Budget

Weekly	Income	Expenses
Salary	$1,000	
Second Job		
Other Income 1	$100	
Other income 2		
Total Income	$1,100	
Gift for God		$250
Rent		$250
Allowance for Self		$100
Allowance for Spouse		$100
Fuel for Car		$50
Telephone		$50
Food		$200
Electric Bill		$30
Savings		$40
Total Expenses		$1,070
Loose Income		$30

Chapter 15
Providing For Your Family

When we become Christians, we embrace the teaching that God and our spiritual family takes precedence over our physical family. (Matthew 12:46-50,10:34-37; Luke 9:59-60) However, this does not mean that we do not love or take care of our own families, no matter how much they may be against our decision to be a Christian.

Anyone who does not provide for their relatives, and especially for their own household, has denied the faith and is worse than an unbeliever. (1 Timothy 5:8)

While it falls on the church to look after those in the church that need help and are really in need (James 1:27, 1 Timothy 5:16), it is our responsibility to look after our own family members such as our parents, grandparents and other relatives.

But if a widow has children or grandchildren, these should learn first of all to put their religion into practice by caring for their own family and so repaying their parents and grandparents, for this is pleasing to God. (1 Timothy 5:4)

"Honor your father and mother" which is the first commandment with a promise *"so that it may go well with you and that you may enjoy long life on the earth."* (Ephesians 6:2-3)

It is sad today that so many people see caring for their parents and other family members – in their old age or in difficult situations – no longer as an obligation. Sadly, some even justify their lack of willingness to love them with all sorts of unbiblical reasoning. This was the same sin that Jesus challenged the Pharisees on in Matthew 15:1-

9 and Mark 7:6-13, as they had set up a tradition of Corban to get out of the responsibility of looking after their parents. In so doing this, *"they nullified the Word of God"* in their lives and became hypocrites.

The ailments of the elderly can be viewed as burdens rather than blessings and opportunities. Too often when the aged need care, we quickly forget the years of sacrifice our parents or grandparents made for us when we were young. Instead of taking them into our homes (whenever this is safe and feasible), some place their aged relatives into retirement communities or nursing homes against their will. On the other hand, it is true that not all elderly people want or need constant, live-in care in their children's homes. They may wish to live with other people their own age in a community, or they may be capable of complete independence. Regardless of the circumstances, we still have obligations to our parents. If they need financial assistance, we should help them. If they are sick, we should take care of them. If they need a place to stay, we should offer our home. If they need help with household work or gardening, we should help them. If they do wish to be in a retirement home or in care, we still need to make sure they are being cared for lovingly.

Many of our parents who are not open to the Gospel will not come to church. Heartbreakingly, they will not let themselves be loved or to see the love of God through disciples. However, God has a great plan, as our parent age they need our help more, and if they move in with us they will see the love of the disciples who visit our homes, attend meetings and overhear the Word of God by default! God loves everyone and wants all to be saved. When we pass up the opportunity to love our parent in their old age, we also often pass up the opportunity to help save their souls.

We must not give into the fear that an opportunity to love our aged parents more will compromise our quality of life. We do not allow ourselves to think like this when we have children, nor should we think like this when we take in our parents.

Jesus and the Apostles set the example in this. In His dying breaths, Jesus cared for His mother and made sure that she was provided for after He had gone. He instructed the Apostle John to take care of her and without hesitation John moved Mary into his home that very day to take care of her.

> *When Jesus saw His mother there, and the disciple whom He loved standing nearby, He said to her, "Woman, here is your son," and to the disciple, "Here is your mother." From that time on, this disciple took her into his home.*
> (John 19:26-27)

Not only are we to provide for our elderly family, but we also are to provide for our children, not only by bringing them up in a manner worthy of respect (1 Timothy 3:4-5) and instructing them in the right ways of life (Proverbs 22:6), but also by financially providing for them by saving up for their needs in the future.

> *Now I am ready to visit you for the third time, and I will not be a burden to you, because what I want is not your possessions but you. After all, children should not have to save up for their parents, but parents for their children.*
> (2 Corinthians 12:14)

One of the longest conversions that I had the privilege to be a part of was with a disciple in the church in Birmingham, England. When Bob was a disciple in his 40's and then into his 50's, he faithfully brought his father Sid to church every week. Bob had him over for Sunday lunch and always talked about the sermon. After seven long years, Sid's heart was softened by consistently hearing the Word of God and sensing Bob's constant love. If you could ask Bob if all the serving, driving, caring, feeding, listening and debating was worth it when he baptized his ailing father, Bob would tell you that there has never been a more special baptism!

Chapter 16
Buying A House And Inheriting Houses

Many disciples ask if it is wise or even allowed to buy a house as a Christian or as an employee of the church. When we look at the leaders of the early church we see that Philip the Evangelist had a house for his family, while the Apostle Paul at times rented a house.

> *Leaving the next day, we reached Caesarea and stayed at the house of Philip the Evangelist, one of the Seven. He had four unmarried daughters who prophesied.* (Acts 21:8-9)

> *For two whole years Paul stayed there in his own rented house and welcomed all who came to see him.* (Acts 28:30)

Buying a house is certainly not wrong as the Bible says houses are inherited and the early church met in homes.

> *Houses and wealth are inherited from parents, but a prudent wife is from the Lord.* (Proverbs 19:14)

> *To Philemon our dear friend and fellow worker, also to Apphia our sister and Archippus our fellow soldier and to the church that meets in your home.* (Philemon 1:1a-2)

The issue is not so much, can I buy a house, but should I at this time and what type? I have seen some Christians buy houses and it hindered them spiritually, but I have also witnessed others buy houses and it helped them tremendously.

> *The wind blows wherever it pleases. You hear its sound, but you cannot tell where it comes from or where it is going. So it is with everyone born of the Spirit.* (John 3:8)

We do not know where God will call us at any given time. While we crave security, and the world tells us security is in owning your own home, this is not true. Our security is in God. If you buy a house that you cannot leave in an instant, then this house has the potential to stop you doing the will of God. This happened to me when I bought into the "Australian dream" and bought a house according to the salary I was making in 2008. When I was called by God to move to another country, the monthly mortgage payments were bigger than the rent we could get for the house, so we could not rent it out and then could not sell it. This in turn led to me delaying God's will for me to move, which in turn led to me and my family struggling spiritually. It would be unwise to buy a house which you cannot rent out quickly and cover your bills or sell quickly. We are meant to live as aliens on this earth, not as permanent residents.

> *All these people were still living by faith when they died. They did not receive the things promised; they only saw them and welcomed them from a distance. And they admitted that they were aliens and strangers on earth.* (Hebrews 11:13)

Is it wise to buy a house so you can live rent free in your old age? It has been for many. However, you should not buy a house if it stops your ability to move where God wants you to and when He wants you to. With that said, we must always deal with the worldliness in our hearts and not crave what our non-Christian friends have or recommend from a non-spiritual perspective. Buying a house that needs a lot of maintaining or renovating would not be a wise decision as a Christian.

Buying a house far from the meetings of the church would not be wise. This makes it difficult to practice hospitality (Romans 12:13 & 16:23) and for you to go and serve others due to the distance. Like most decisions in life, it is the spiritual aspects that we must consider more than the wants, as it says in Corinthians:

"Everything is permissible" but not everything is beneficial. "Everything is permissible" but not everything is constructive. Nobody should seek his own good, but the good of others." (1 Corinthians 10:23-24)

Some of us may inherit houses or land. I would suggest the same principles apply: Does looking after it help or hinder your spiritual life? The Old Testament has many things to say about inheritances, but in context, these were to be lands given to children that were originally given by God to His people that were not meant to be taken away. (Ezekiel 46:16-18; Micah 2:1-2) As Christians, we are no longer a physical nation like Israel, so this does not apply. Additionally, when Jesus was asked to deal with such an issue, He focused on the heart.

Someone in the crowd said to Him, "Teacher, tell my brother to divide the inheritance with me."

Jesus replied, "Man, who appointed me a judge or an arbiter between you?" Then He said to them, "Watch out! Be on your guard against all kinds of greed; life does not consist in an abundance of possessions."

And Jesus told them this parable: "The ground of a certain rich man yielded an abundant harvest. He thought to himself, 'What shall I do? I have no place to store my crops.' "Then he said, 'This is what I'll do. I will tear down my barns and build bigger ones, and there I will store my surplus grain. And I'll say to myself, "You have plenty of grain laid up for many years. Take life easy; eat, drink and be merry."'

"But God said to him, 'You fool! This very night your life will be demanded from you. Then who will get what you have prepared for yourself?" This is how it will be with whoever stores up things for themselves but is not rich toward God. (Luke 12:13-21)

Our focus should not be on gaining and expanding our wealth or acquiring a string of properties. We are to live for today and wisely plan for tomorrow, so as not to be a burden on others (2 Thessalonians 3:7-9) and to be rich toward God. If you come into wealth, do not go out and buy more possessions just because you can. If a property is easily managed and does not distract you spiritually, emotionally or financially, then it may be a great asset for the future. However, consider with your new-found wealth how you can be generous toward God. Could you use some of the money to further His Kingdom or provide free housing for a minister, therefore again helping the church financially? It is all about your heart toward God. Be rich toward God and do not be distracted. (Mark 4:18-19)

Chapter 17
What Career Should I Choose?

Then I realized that it is good and proper for a man to eat and drink, and to find satisfaction in his toilsome labor under the sun during the few days of life God has given him, for this is his lot. Moreover, when God gives any man wealth and possessions, and enables him to enjoy them, to accept his lot and be happy in his work, this is a gift of God. He seldom reflects on the days of his life, because God keeps him occupied with gladness of heart. I have seen another evil under the sun, and it weighs heavily on men: God gives a man wealth, possessions and honor, so that he lacks nothing his heart desires, but God does not enable him to enjoy them, and a stranger enjoys them instead. This is meaningless, a grievous evil. (Ecclesiastes 5:18-6:2)

I worked in recruitment for many years and have interviewed countless amounts of people. When people come to you as a recruitment agent, they tend to be more open with you than with a company because they know you have many job options with many companies. One of the first questions that I would ask the applicant was, "What is the ideal job for which you are looking?"

People's answers rarely contain the sort of job they want, but contain what is important to them practically such as: I want this much money; these certain hours so I can get home to my kids; this close to home as I do not want to be stuck in traffic; a job that is not behind a desk, so I do not get fat; etc. When people start to choose a career at the beginning of their life, they rarely take these following aspects into consideration: The ungodly hours that a certain career requires; the amount of time away from family; or how it will affect your health over a long period of time.

When I was sixteen and deciding upon a career, I did not have a clue as to what I really wanted to do. I thought about what I enjoyed and thought it should be based on that. I loved to cook and then my grandmother mentioned that I would make a good hotel manager when she saw me in a suit one day. That was good enough for me. I then pursued a career in hospitality, one of the worst paying industries you can get into in my country! The other downfalls of the industry were: that it has one of the worse schedules often with split shifts; you are around food all day; and the industry is known for a high divorce rate. That is not to say you cannot pursue that career, but simply as an example to get you to really think before choosing a career only based on what you enjoy.

God wants us to be happy and find satisfaction in the job we do. However, the things that make Christians happy in the long run have more to do with having time to read their Bibles and pray before they run off to work; being able to get home in time to spend time with their children before they go to bed; having weekends free to spend time with other Christians and friends they want to help become Christians; sociable hours that free you up to not miss church meetings or social events; and especially a job that does not tempt you to fall into sin or compromise your devotion to God and His Kingdom.

Before making a huge decision about what career you should choose, look around and see who has a happy spiritual life. What careers have they chosen? Check to see if there are many spiritual Christians in the career you are considering. Consider the location of the kind of job for which you are looking. Are the potential roles plentiful in cities where there are churches? Is your chosen industry known for being well paid for sociable hours? How much debt will you have after university if you study this discipline and how quickly will you be able to pay it off?

Some of the most idolized jobs, such as doctors, lawyers and solicitors are also jobs that may not allow you the freedom to spend quality time loving God and loving your neighbor. This does depend a large amount on your specialization within that field. Consider carefully, with your spirituality and salvation in mind, before throwing yourself into a career. If you live in a third world economy, it is important that you go to college, if you get the opportunity, because good jobs that give you the flexibility to spend time in the Kingdom and with your family are usually only found in this circle. Otherwise you might be working for almost nothing Monday through Saturday. Also consider that being in a campus ministry is often one of the best ways to grow spiritually.

You must really count the cost if working while engaged in your studies is necessary. Often in the third world, it is the only way to get ahead in life, but that means that you might work from 9am to 6pm and then go to school from 7pm to 10pm. Many who do this fall away as they are tempted to miss meetings of the body and find in hard to feel the love of the disciples because of their limited time. They hear all the challenges, but do not make themselves available for the love and support needed to handle those challenges. If this is the case, you should consider one or the other. Never forget: God and your salvation come first. It is better to remain poor and go to Heaven than to try to better yourself financially and fall away.

Those who want to get rich fall into temptation and a trap and into many foolish and harmful desires that plunge people into ruin and destruction. For the love of money is a root of all kinds of evil. Some people, eager for money, have wandered from the faith and pierced themselves with many griefs. (1 Timothy 10:23-24)

I have also seen the opposite. I have seen disciples fall away because they did not further their careers and make the temporary time sacrifices that were necessary. They gave into bitterness from envy and jealousy at what others had or had accomplished. Every person's case is different, much advice must be sought from God and older Christians who have the wisdom to instruct in these areas. God simply calls us to be happy with our lot in life. (Luke 3:14; Philippians 4:11-13)

Chapter 18
How To Make Money

A kindhearted woman gains respect, but ruthless men gain only wealth. (Proverbs 11:16)

There are many ways to make money but beware as some are ungodly. We will talk about how the godly should make money, because it is better to be righteous and poor than unrighteous and wealthy.

Better a poor man whose walk is blameless than a fool whose lips are perverse. (Proverbs 19:1)

A fortune made by a lying tongue is a fleeting vapor and a deadly snare. (Proverbs 21:6)

The following are a few keys:

A. Hard Work And Diligence

Lazy hands make a man poor, but diligent hands bring wealth. (Proverbs 10:4)

All hard work brings a profit, but mere talk leads only to poverty. (Proverbs 14:23)

He who works his land will have abundant food, but he who chases fantasies lacks judgment. (Proverbs 12:11)

From the fruit of his lips a man is filled with good things as surely as the work of his hands rewards him. (Proverbs 12:14)

Diligent hands will rule, but laziness ends in slave labor.
(Proverbs 12:24)

A little sleep, a little slumber, a little folding of the hands to rest – and poverty will come on you like a bandit and scarcity like an armed man. (Proverbs 24:33-34)

Many people do not think that they are lazy when in reality they are, because they compare themselves with themself or other lazy people. You may be less lazy than you were last week or last year, but that does not mean you are a hard worker. Lazy people often feel like other people's standard of hard work, especially what it takes to achieve success, are unrealistic and even harsh. Jesus addressed this issue in the Parable of the Talents in Matthew 25:

Again, it will be like a man going on a journey, who called his servants and entrusted his property to them. To one he gave five talents of money, to another two talents, and to another one talent, each according to his ability. Then he went on his journey. The man who had received the five talents went at once and put his money to work and gained five more. So also, the one with the two talents gained two more. But the man who had received the one talent went off, dug a hole in the ground and hid his master's money.

After a long time the master of those servants returned and settled accounts with them. The man who had received the five talents brought the other five. "Master," he said, "you entrusted me with five talents. See, I have gained five more."

His master replied, "Well done, good and faithful

servant! You have been faithful with a few things; I will put you in charge of many things. Come and share your master's happiness!" The man with the two talents also came. "Master," he said, "you entrusted me with two talents; see, I have gained two more." His master replied, "Well done, good and faithful servant! You have been faithful with a few things; I will put you in charge of many things. Come and share your master's happiness!"

Then the man who had received the one talent came. "Master," he said, "I knew that you are a hard man, harvesting where you have not sown and gathering where you have not scattered seed. So I was afraid and went out and hid your talent in the ground. See, here is what belongs to you." His master replied, "You wicked, lazy servant! So you knew that I harvest where I have not sown and gather where I have not scattered seed? Well then, you should have put my money on deposit with the bankers, so that when I returned I would have received it back with interest."

"Take the talent from him and give it to the one who has the ten talents. For everyone who has will be given more, and he will have an abundance. Whoever does not have, even what he has will be taken from him. And throw that worthless servant outside, into the darkness, where there will be weeping and gnashing of teeth."
(Matthew 25:14-30)

When we work hard, and have God with us as Christians, in the long run it will produce wealth. If we are not producing wealth over an extended period, then we must ask ourselves how hard we are really working?

B. A Consistent Plan

Dishonest money dwindles away, but he who gathers money little by little makes it grow. (Proverbs 13:11)

He who ignores discipline comes to poverty and shame, but whoever heeds correction is honored.
(Proverbs 13:18)

Here we find for the lazy, the dreaded principle of consistency; not just a one-off event, but every day, every week and every year. My daughter says, "One salad does not make you thin and one donut does not make you fat." In the same way, one good decision with wealth does not secure your greater wealth. It is only after many, many good decisions that more wealth will be accumulated. You need to save to produce capital, to give yourself cash flow, which in turn gives you the money to gain more wealth. This also has spiritual implications. If you want to know how to be trusted with spiritual things, start with managing your money well, as Jesus talks about in the Parable of the Shrewd Manager in Luke 16.

Whoever can be trusted with very little can also be trusted with much, and whoever is dishonest with very little will also be dishonest with much. (Luke 16:10)

C. Righteousness

Misfortune pursues the sinner but prosperity is the reward of the righteous. (Proverbs 13:21)

Humility and the fear of the Lord bring wealth and honor and life. (Proverbs 22:4)

Having worked in the corporate world, it continues to amaze me to see how shallow people are. I saw so many people who wanted to get rich quick and not build their reputation on good service. This may be attributed to the fact that people do not stay with one company very long any more. In the business that I was in, there was a large sales component, and most sales people do not speak "the truth, the whole truth and nothing but the truth." As a result, their clients are not loyal to them and what was once their best client often leaves them, creating a greater need to sell. Consequently, the cycle goes around and around. In a world consumed with instant success, instant wealth and instant satisfaction, many simply never gain wealth because they compromise their righteousness. This not only defiles their hearts and consciences, but also does not work long term. Be completely honest. Own your mistakes and never cover them up and let God work.

D. Wisdom

By wisdom a house is built, and through understanding it is established; through knowledge its rooms are filled with rare and beautiful treasures. (Proverbs 24:3-4)

He who works his land will have abundant food, but the one who chases fantasies will have his fill of poverty. (Proverbs 28:19)

Wealth is not simply about hard work. You can work hard digging for treasure, but if you are in the wrong spot your hard work amounts to nothing. You need hard work applied to the right knowledge. Unfortunately, those with that knowledge are so busy working that they are not that accessible. To get that knowledge, you need to read the right books and be mentored by the right people. The best business book in the world is the Bible! Within the pages of Proverbs are most of the business principles you will ever need. Within the Books of Kings and Chronicles there are more stories on leadership, good and bad, than you could ever need. As for building a chain of global outlets that effectively gets people to buy into changing their lives for something at great cost, you do not need to look further than imitating Jesus and "His employees" who built a worldwide movement. When applying these principles to our modern world, they still work, especially if you couple them with up-to-date knowledge from recent successful businesses. Learn to make good decisions based on knowledge and not emotions. Deal in facts not feelings. Get lots and lots of advice from successful people and your hard work will be rewarded.

> *Plans fail for lack of counsel, but with many advisers they succeed.* (Proverbs 15:22)

E. Tips

As I mentioned earlier, I spent many years working in recruitment, interviewing people from many different industries on their way out of a job and company, then placing them into new companies and new jobs. Here are some tips that I have learned from all those interviews, meeting with different companies and hiring managers.

1. A person's pay has less to do with their skill and more to do with the company's product, so pick the right company whose products cost little to make. An example would be selling drinks. Coke pays well as opposed to milk companies because Coke costs

little to make and milk costs a lot to make. And both companies sell drinks.

2. It is often wise to look for a better job even when you are in a happy one, as your career will go much, much faster.

3. If you do not ask for a raise in salary, you will rarely get one or the one that you could.

4. Make your role indispensable. If you become an expert in an area in the business no one else wants to do, you will be the last person they look to get rid of and the first they will reward.

5. Happiness in a role has more to do with needs than wants. Why are you looking to leave? What are you looking for in a new role?

6. The better a job, the less people apply for it. So apply for jobs you do not think you can get.

7. Become your boss' friend. Friends rarely fire friends.

8. Medium sized, owner operated businesses normally give the best rewards and opportunities. Small companies measure money by personal decisions. I "cannot" give him a pay rise of $10,000, I would rather buy my daughter a car. Large businesses have policies that band salaries and benefits by policies that they cannot break.

9. When changing jobs, switch between companies with a recognized brand name. Then switch to a company without one who pays you well because you worked for a branded name company. Then switch back to a branded name. This is a quicker way to increase your pay and gain a more recognized job title.

10. Always ask your boss what you need to do to get your next pay raise and do what they say as quickly as you can.

11. Keep up with the job market expectations. Look up on the internet topics such as "Unique Ways to Score A Job Interview," "Preparing for An Interview," "Helpful Tips for An Interview," "How to Secure A Job After University When Others Do Not," "How to Sell Yourself in An Interview." There is so much good stuff on the Internet that has been researched by specialists and is up to date. Never forget to be current.

Chapter 19
Savings, Retirement And Leaving An Inheritance

Laughing At The Days To Come

She brings him good, not harm, all the days of her life. She selects wool and flax and works with eager hands. She is like the merchant ships, bringing her food from afar. She gets up while it is still night; she provides food for her family and portions for her female servants. She considers a field and buys it; out of her earnings she plants a vineyard. She sets about her work vigorously; her arms are strong for her tasks. She sees that her trading is profitable, and her lamp does not go out at night. In her hand she holds the distaff and grasps the spindle with her fingers. She opens her arms to the poor and extends her hands to the needy. When it snows, she has no fear for her household; for all of them are clothed in scarlet. She makes coverings for her bed; she is clothed in fine linen and purple. Her husband is respected at the city gate, where he takes his seat among the elders of the land. She makes linen garments and sells them, and supplies the merchants with sashes. She is clothed with strength and dignity; she can laugh at the days to come. (Proverbs 31:12-25)

This passage talks about the wife of noble character. When she thinks of the days to come, she laughs at them! Why? Because she is hard working, industrious and entrepreneurial. She has a life that thinks about the future, thinks about the needs of her family, future problems or needs that might occur, and plans to provide for them. We can learn a lot form her attitude and example.

Some have asked, "Are savings good, allowed and godly? Or should we give it all to God and His work now?" When we look at the

Scriptures we see that we are encouraged to grow and save our wealth and to leave an inheritance for our children.

A good man leaves an inheritance for his children's children, but a sinner's wealth is stored up for the righteous. (Proverbs 13:22)

Wisdom, like an inheritance, is a good thing and benefits those who see the sun. (Ecclesiastes 7:11)

Houses and wealth are inherited from parents, but a prudent wife is from the Lord. (Proverbs 19:14)

Now I am ready to visit you for the third time, and I will not be a burden to you, because what I want is not your possessions but you. After all, children should not have to save up for their parents, but parents for their children. So I will very gladly spend for you everything I have and expend myself as well. If I love you more, will you love me less? (2 Corinthians 12:14-15)

You must build your wealth to look after yourself in your old age and pass that wealth down to your children so that you do not put the responsibility of looking after yourself on your children. Ideally, you do not want to have to depend on anyone else.

Make it your ambition to lead a quiet life, to mind your own business and to work with your hands, just as we told you, so that your daily life may win the respect of outsiders and so that you will not be dependent on anybody.
(1 Thessalonians 4:11-1

Like most things, the "secret" of building wealth is to do it consistently *"little by little."* My father says that you either work hard early in life or late in life. His meaning is that if you do not get the principle of working hard and saving wealth when you are young, you will at the end of your life because it will be forced on you by necessity. Many people when they are young and have few bills, squander their wealth. Then when they get married and have kids, they find it hard to save because they now have more bills. They also want to live the lavish life they once lived before they had a family. They then fall into debt and struggle to get out of it for the rest of their life. The encouragement in the Scriptures is make providing for yourself in the future a consistent thing throughout your life. Do it consistently and after you saved small amounts over a long period, you will have gained a substantial amount.

> *In the house of the wise are stores of choice food and oil, but a foolish man devours all he has.* (Proverbs 21:20)

> *Dishonest money dwindles away, but he who gathers money little by little makes it grow.* (Proverbs 13:11)

Some are confused about how these principles line up against Scriptures that talk about not storing up treasures on earth and using your money to win souls.

> *Do not store up for yourselves treasures on earth, where moth and rust destroy, and where thieves break in and steal. But store up for yourselves treasures in Heaven, where moth and rust do not destroy, and where thieves do not break in and steal. For where your treasure is, there your heart will be also.* (Matthew 6:19-21)

I tell you, use worldly wealth to gain friends for yourselves, so that when it is gone, you will be welcomed into eternal dwellings. (Luke 16:9)

The issue is needs versus wants. Storing up treasures is very different from providing for your needs. Having enough to live on and using your excess to win friends to Christ are not in contradiction. A Christian should live a simple life so that others can simply live, and that simple life should be lived to the end. Filling our life with possessions and grand schemes of our retirement life is not what Christ lived for and nor should we.

When a Christian and a non-Christian think of retirement, they usually think of it in two very different ways. In one sense, a Christian does not think of retiring at all, as our mission is to save as many as possible for the whole of our life, so sitting back, drinking cocktails and doing nothing is not a Christian's idea of retirement. Yet as we get older, we will through age and diminishing health, be able to do less and less. So, in that sense, we need to plan to provide for this eventuality. God gives us an insight into this with his priests in the Old Testament.

The Lord said to Moses, "This applies to the Levites: Men twenty-five years old or more shall come to take part in the work at the Tent of Meeting, but at the age of fifty, they must retire from their regular service and work no longer. They may assist their brothers in performing their duties at the Tent of Meeting, but they themselves must not do the work. This, then, is how you are to assign the responsibilities of the Levites." (Numbers 8:23-26)

Practicals Of Planning For The Future

There is an array of books on how to save for retirement written by non-Christians. There is a lot of good information as well as information and advice that will turn out to not help you, as economic climates and laws change over the course of decades. Here are some tips that are consistent:

1. Buy a house that you can pay off in your lifetime instead of paying rent, so that you live rent free for as many years as possible, especially during your retirement when your income is usually less than your working years.
2. If you can buy a house and pay it off earlier on in life, buy a second house very close to you and pay that off so you can use the rent you get from it as your future income. For needed income if a second house is impossible to buy, you could convert a room or garage in your house to rent out.
3. Save for your retirement. While this is unsure as most pension funds are subjects to other people controlling them, the stock market and other things, it is still good to save. However, it is best not to rely on it as the only way to support yourself.
4. Constantly "Up Skill" yourself in different income streams and careers. This way as your health diminishes, you are still very employable. Some examples are writing, editing, proof reading, baking, making things you can sell at markets or on the Internet, jobs that let you work at your own pace, the list is endless. Start researching them on the Internet.
5. Love your children and teach them to work hard by your example. The by-product, but not the reason for doing this, is that they will cost you less financially, as being a hard worker often enables children to get scholarships for education and stay away from sin that ultimately costs them and you financially.
6. Learn to live a simple and joyful life now, so that you do not

need as much money in your retirement.

7. Keep in good health so that your medical bills are low and your ability to work is long lasting. Exercise, daily if possible. Keep your weight at the medically recommended weight.

Last but not least:

8. Always stay spiritual and righteous. The ultimate solution is to have God take care of you as He has promised to do.

> *I was young and now I am old, yet I have never seen the righteous forsaken or their children begging bread.*
> (Psalms 37:25)

My wealth and therefore that of my wife has fluctuated throughout our lives. At points, it has been very little due to sacrificing for the Kingdom, and we have been tempted to feel insecure at times and ask, "So what if all goes wrong?" Christians know that we are commanded to not worry or give into fear because God will look after us (Matthew 6:24-34). For most, that can be easier said than done. "What if it all goes wrong?" Those who I thought would look after me do not or die. "What if the plans I make go wrong?" One story that helps my heart is that of the prophet's family in Elisha's time.

> *The wife of a man from the company of the prophets cried out to Elisha, "Your servant my husband is dead, and you know that he revered the Lord. But now his creditor is coming to take my two boys as his slaves."*
>
> *Elisha replied to her, "How can I help you? Tell me, what do you have in your house?" "Your servant has nothing there at all," she said, "except a little oil."*
> *Elisha said, "Go around and ask all your neighbors for*

empty jars. Don't ask for just a few. Then go inside and shut the door behind you and your sons. Pour oil into all the jars, and as each is filled, put it to one side."

She left him and afterward shut the door behind her and her sons. They brought the jars to her and she kept pouring. When all the jars were full, she said to her son, "Bring me another one."

But he replied, "There is not a jar left." Then the oil stopped flowing. She went and told the man of God, and he said, "Go, sell the oil and pay your debts. You and your sons can live on what is left." (2 Kings 4:1-7)

It does not say why this prophet was in debt or why he died. What it does tell us is that a righteous man, whose humble and solution-orientated wife sought advice from a godly man. He then gave her a plan that took faith and action on her part. As she humbly worked hard to obey the instruction, God brought about a miracle that demonstrates to us His love for His righteous prophet and his family. This account helps my heart, because I am sure that the prophet never considered that upon his death, he would leave his wife in such a desperate situation as the creditors would take their boys. With that said, the worst almost happened, yet God – as He has promised us all – took care of the widow and her sons. It also shows the need for husbands to teach their wives to always look to God in times of need.

Chapter 20
Lending, Borrowing Money And Dealing With Debts

Under the Old Covenant, when Israel was a physical nation, God's people lent each other money rather than having a brother borrow money from a non-believer. However, unlike the unbeliever, they were not to charge interest on any loan to their brother. (Deuteronomy 23:19-20) As with all things under the New Covenant, Jesus taught a higher standard.

A. Lending Money

Christians if they chose to lend money should give the money and not expect it back.

> *If you love those who love you, what credit is that to you? Even "sinners" love those who love them. And if you do good to those who are good to you, what credit is that to you? Even "sinners" do that. And if you lend to those from whom you expect repayment, what credit is that to you? Even "sinners" lend to "sinners," expecting to be repaid in full. But love your enemies, do good to them, and lend to them without expecting to get anything back. Then your reward will be great, and you will be sons of the Most High, because He is kind to the ungrateful and wicked. Be merciful, just as your Father is merciful.* (Luke 6:32-36)

If you cannot afford to lose the money that you are considering lending, then you absolutely should not lend the money. This protects your heart from any bitterness if you are not repaid. If it is in your means to "lend" and perhaps "give" money to others, then you should do so willingly.

B. Borrowing Money

No Christian should depend upon another for wealth or means to be supported. (1 Thessalonians 4:11-12) If you are not working, God goes even further and says you should not eat rather than borrow from disciples. (2 Thessalonians 3:10) All debts must be paid to people and authorities except the debt of loved owed to others.

> *This is also why you pay taxes, for the authorities are God's servants, who give their full-time to governing. Give everyone what you owe him: If you owe taxes, pay taxes; if revenue, then revenue; if respect, then respect; if honor, then honor. Let no debt remain outstanding, except the continuing debt to love one another, for he who loves his fellowman has fulfilled the Law.* (Romans 13:6-8)

Borrowing money for wants or pleasures – perhaps even things other people can afford but you cannot like attending events, buying presents, etc. – is not to be done. When Christians borrow money to do things they cannot afford to do, and then cannot pay the lender back, this often causes the lender to struggle emotionally and spiritually. Our society teaches us to buy on credit, to have what we cannot afford. We must not do so. Rather we are to live within our means, even if that causes embarrassment, upsetting others or going without.

C. Dealing With Debt

Some people who become Christians come into the Kingdom with debt. Some Christians through unrighteousness, misfortune or mismanagement also find themselves in debt. So the question comes. "How do deal with these situations?" There are a lot of different ways to deal with debts and it differs in many countries due to the laws, amenities and culture, but here are some tips.

1. Get radical about your debt. Most people get into debt because they overspend. Yet, most are convinced – but deceived – that they do not overspend, or they think they have a right to. You must cut your costs and change your spending habits, avoid eating out, buy cheaper brands of food, etc.

2. Figure out which debt you are paying the most interest on and tackle that debt first as it is costing you the most. Many focus on paying off the smallest debt first as it makes them feel better, as that may then leave them with three not four loans after paying it off. This is not the best financial decision.

3. Get yourself a plan and budget to deal with the debt. You need to see light at the end of the tunnel. Know when you will be out of debt to have something to aim at.

4. Get someone to hold you accountable on a weekly basis with weekly goals about what you spend and your progress in paying off your debt.

5. Look for ways to reduce the interest on your debt; look for better loans with lower fees.

6. Increase your wage, change jobs, get a second job to pay things off quicker.

7. Contact your creditors and ask to be forgiven of your debt. (Yes, I have seen this happen!) Another option is asking them to reduce your debt or fees on your debt.

8. Learn to use only cash instead of credit cards and you will find that you spend less. Kerry and I get our allowances out at the beginning of every month in cash. It stops us spending more when we see the actual cash leave our hands and our monthly allowance diminish visually before our eyes.

9. If credit cards have been a source of your debts, then consider using a debit card and cutting up your credit cards so you cannot use them.

10. Get lots and lots of help. Do not think that by ignoring the problem of debt that it will go away.

The Example Of Brenda.

Kerry and I helped restore a sister to the faith named Brenda a few years ago. She was in her late 30's and was $36,000 AUS in debt. When she tried to deal with her debt, she would look at the numbers, feel so overwhelmed and at a loss with how to deal with it, that she would get a pedicure, go for a nice meal, and watch a movie to make herself feel better, putting her in more debt. I do not think Brenda is an isolated case.

So, Kerry and I asked to help her. We reviewed all her finances, sorted out which credit card had the highest interest, and tackled that one first. We had her live with us, so she did not have to pay rent or bills. (The equivalent may be living back with your parents.) We monitored her spending and income, and just in 18 months, Brenda's debt was down to just over $20,000 AUS.

We then helped her look for a small apartment that she could buy and secure a small mortgage. It was not flash or in the best area, but in Australia, properties at the bottom of the housing market go up in value the fastest.

So, after a year of living in the apartment, the value went up enough for Brenda to remortgage so that she could pay off her high interest debts and bundle her debt into her mortgage, leaving her with one manageable monthly expense with a low interest. On paper, she was completely out of debt just two years later.

It does not matter where you start when dealing with your debt, but you must start to address it before it gets worse.

D. Bankruptcy

Is it ok to declare bankruptcy? A good question to ask. To answer this question, we must ask why does the law of some lands allow businesses to go bankrupt without having to pay back its debts? Let me explain from a true-life case in business.

Fred (not his real name) set up a business and the government even gave Fred tax concessions on his business in the early years to make it easier for Fred to succeed. Fred employed three people at the end of his first year. They all paid taxes to the government. Then by the end of the second year, Fred employed two more people. All five paid taxes to the government. In the third year, Fred employed two more people who all pay taxes to the government, and Fred began paying company taxes to the government. This process went on for ten years, and all the while, every employee paid taxes to the government and Fred paid company taxes for eight years. The total money given to the government by the employees was approximately $950,000 AUS – $100,000 AUS per employee per year. The total money given to the government by the company for eight years of taxes at 30% was about $3,000,000 AUS.

So, the government was given $3,950,000 AUS for doing what? Well, they hire a few people that take a small look at the business taxes that at most takes one person a few weeks, a minimal cost. So, when Fred's business did badly to the point of bankruptcy and could not employ people who pay taxes, that in turn hurt the government's income. When Fred's business went out of business, he could not pay business taxes. So, to keep Fred and his employees paying taxes and giving the government income, the government allowed Fred to declare bankruptcy and start afresh after some limitations. Although the debt that Fred owed the government was $1,000,000 AUS, the government already had been given $3,950,000 AUS in taxes. So now the government's income was down to $2,950,000 AUS. The important thing to the government was to get Fred back in business and employing people so that they could get back to paying their taxes and avoiding them asking the government for money in benefits. So now, after declaring bankruptcy which allowed Fred to start again, his now very profitable company and employees are once again paying taxes to the government.

The world understands the principle and value of bankruptcy. It is purely business, non-emotional facts and figures, just business. It encourages people to risk starting up businesses and fuels the economy. Yet when Christians think of going bankrupt, there is often a shame to it as if they have committed a great sin. There can often be a misplaced self-righteousness or pride that makes some Christians feel like they need to pay back every last penny in situations like this. Maybe Jesus Parable of the Shrewd Manager can help us understand how we can apply this to a person's situation.

> *Jesus told His disciples, "There was a rich man whose manager was accused of wasting his possessions. So he called him in and asked him, 'What is this I hear about you? Give an account of your management, because you cannot be manager any longer.'"*

> *"The manager said to himself, 'What shall I do now? My master is taking away my job. I'm not strong enough to dig, and I'm ashamed to beg, I know what I'll do so that, when I lose my job here, people will welcome me into their houses.'"*

> *"So he called in each one of his master's debtors. He asked the first, 'How much do you owe my master?'" "'Nine hundred gallons of olive oil,' he replied."*

"The manager told him, 'Take your bill, sit down quickly, and make it four hundred and fifty.'"

"Then he asked the second, 'And how much do you owe?'" "'A thousand bushels of wheat,' he replied." "He told him, 'Take your bill and make it eight hundred.'"

"The master commended the dishonest manager because he had acted shrewdly. For the people of this world are more shrewd in dealing with their own kind than are the people of the light. I tell you, use worldly wealth to gain friends for yourselves, so that when it is gone, you will be welcomed into eternal dwellings."

"Whoever can be trusted with very little can also be trusted with much, and whoever is dishonest with very little will also be dishonest with much. So if you have not been trustworthy in handling worldly wealth, who will trust you with true riches? And if you have not been trustworthy with someone else's property, who will give you property of your own?"

"No one can serve two masters. Either you will hate the one and love the other, or you will be devoted to the one and despise the other. You cannot serve both God and Money.

The Pharisees, who loved money, heard all this and were sneering at Jesus. He said to them, 'You are the ones who justify yourselves in the eyes of others, but God knows your hearts. What people value highly is detestable in God's sight.'" (Luke 16:1-15)

At first it seems that Jesus is commending the dishonest manager for lying and stealing. Yet what Jesus is alluding to is that non-spiritual people are often more clued in to how the world works than spiritual people are and therefore they miss God-given opportunities. If the government you live under allows you to declare bankruptcy legally, either as a business owner or in your own personal financial situation, enabling you to get back on your feet and pay your taxes, do it. If this in turn helps your spouse to work and pay taxes and not claim benefits, do it. If it allows your children to then have a fresh start and be able to earn money so they can pay taxes, it is shrewd to take what your government has made part of the law, to help you along the way in life.

Now we cannot be bad-hearted and plan to aim for bankruptcy by overspending. God is watching and deals with everyone according to their righteousness. However, on the other side of the coin, we are not to be so proud as to not received the help afforded us. We must focus on being justified before God not concerned about misguided disciples who "look down" on bankruptcy. When we learn from our mistakes and how to get out of them, we in turn can help so many.

Chapter 21
Should I Pay Taxes To An Unjust Government?

Over the years, I have heard some Christians ask why they should pay taxes to a government with which they have strong ideological disagreements. Their justifications to not pay taxes range from their political policies to the fact that they are being persecuted by their government. To find the answer to this question, we should go to an instance where Jesus was questioned about this matter.

> *Later they sent some of the Pharisees and Herodians to Jesus to catch Him in His words. They came to Him and said, "Teacher, we know you are a man of integrity. You aren't swayed by men, because you pay no attention to who they are; but you teach the way of God in accordance with the truth. Is it right to pay taxes to Caesar or not? Should we pay or shouldn't we?"*
>
> *But Jesus knew their hypocrisy. "Why are you trying to trap me?" He asked. "Bring me a denarius and let me look at it." They brought the coin, and He asked them, "Whose portrait is this? And whose inscription?"*
>
> *"Caesar's," they replied. Then Jesus said to them, "Give to Caesar what is Caesar's and to God what is God's." And they were amazed at Him."* (Mark 12:13-17)

The Jews saw themselves as governed by an unjust government, the Romans. In this passage, Jesus clearly teaches that we should support them, even though He knew it was the Romans that would later kill Him. He even gave the Temple tax. (Also see Matthew 17:24-7; Luke 20:20-26; Matthew 22:15-22) This principle is again reiterated by Paul to the Christians in Rome, the heart of political power of the Roman Empire and a city full of false gods and immoral practices.

This is also why you pay taxes, for the authorities are God's servants, who give their full-time to governing. Give to everyone what you owe them: If you owe taxes, pay taxes; if revenue, then revenue; if respect, then respect; if honor, then honor. (Romans 13:6-7)

Jesus was known for His integrity in all things, including taxes. We must make sure that when we do our taxes today that we are completely honest, not bending the truth to get more money back from the government than we should.

Conclusion

Of making many books there is no end, and much study wearies the body. Now all has been heard; here I the conclusion of the matter: Fear God and keep His commandments, for this is the duty of all mankind. For God will bring every deed into judgement, including every hidden thing, whether it is good or evil.
(Ecclesiastes 12:12b-14)

This Scripture was written by one of the richest men that ever lived, King Solomon. This was his incredibly brief, simple and yet profound conclusion given at the end of his life. The Scripture that I have used with my own heart on the matter is in 1 John. To me it gave me a clear choice in my beliefs, do I believe God loves me and that He will take care of my every need no matter how generous I am? Or do I live like an unbeliever, trying to control my life by living by sight and not faith?

And so we know and rely on the love God has for us. For God is love. (1 John 1:16a)

Either God exists and loves me, so everything will be ok, or there is no God and we are all in trouble. I must choose daily which I will believe, for there is no middle ground! It is my hope that in reading this book, you have been convinced that simply obeying God, being generous on all occasions, and trusting God's promises to provide for you, is the only way to live. My dear father, Stephen Willis, instilled in me the generosity of God by his consistent example. Thanks Dad! My passionate mother, Rosemary Willis, demonstrated that constantly talking about God and His Scriptures seems crazy to others, but there is no other way for people around you to get God's message. Thanks Mum!

I am humbled to say that their example has led me to keep God's commands. This simple call to **"Fear God and keep His commandments"** coupled with the enthusiasm of the love of my life, Kerry, has led to both of our kids becoming incredibly generous in all their dealings. All four of us are living a blessed life.

Who you are, and your deep convictions greatly influence not only how your life goes, but all those around you, especially you children. So, it is imperative that we quickly and steadfastly grasp God's mindset on money. For the decisions you make today will be felt for eternity!

> *Wealth and honor come from you; you are the ruler of all things. In your hands are strength and power to exalt and give strength to all.* (Ecclesiastes 12:12b-14)

To God always be the glory for ever more! So be it!